DATE DUE

The Past in Ruins

A VOLUME IN THE SERIES

CRITICAL PERSPECTIVES ON MODERN CULTURE

EDITED BY DAVID GROSS AND

WILLIAM M. JOHNSTON

DAVID GROSS

The Past in Ruins

TRADITION AND THE
CRITIQUE OF MODERNITY

THE UNIVERSITY OF MASSACHUSETTS PRESS

AMHERST

Copyright © 1992 by
The University of Massachusetts Press
All rights reserved
Printed in the United States of America
LC 92–10935
ISBN 0–87023–821–3
Designed by Dorothy Thompson Griffin
Typeset by Keystone Typesetting in Linotron Primer
Printed and bound by Thomson-Shore

Library of Congress Cataloging-in-Publication Data
Gross, David, 1940–
    The past in ruins : tradition and the critique of modernity /
    David Gross.
        p.   .cm. — (Critical perspectives on modern culture)
    Includes bibliographical references and index.
    ISBN 0–87023–821–3 (alk. paper)
    1. Civilization, Modern—Philosophy.   2. Tradition (Philosophy)
I. Title.   II. Series.
CB358.G76   1992
901—dc20   92–10935
                                                          CIP

British Library Cataloguing in Publication data are available.

In memory of my father

Only the gaze that is turned backward
can bring us forward,
for the gaze that is turned forward
leads us backward.

NOVALIS

Contents

Acknowledgments

I want to express my gratitude to Paul Breines, Will Johnston, Bill Martin, and Alan Megill for their careful reading of this book in manuscript form, and for their many helpful suggestions. I greatly appreciated the enthusiasm that Clark Dougan of the University of Massachusetts Press showed for this work from the beginning, and I am indebted to Carol Schoen for her skillful job of copyediting. But my sincerest thanks go, yet again, to Ruthanne, Stefan, and David for their unfailing patience and support. This book is for them.

The Past in Ruins

Introduction

Tradition has been central to human life for millennia. Its main function has been to provide the values, beliefs, and guidelines for conduct that have helped mold communities into organic wholes. It has also been the crucial force providing linkage from one generation to the next. Where animals have had instinct to bind them together, human beings have had tradition. From the very earliest tribal and communal beginnings down to the advent of the modern age, tradition has always been present as virtual second nature. Without it there would have been no effective social integration, nor any connecting tissue holding together, in Edmund Burke's words, "those who are living, those who are dead, and those who are [yet] to be born."[1]

It is also true that for at least as long as there have been written records there have been complaints that tradition has not been given due respect. Some of the most ancient Egyptian and Near Eastern texts indicate a concern that the "old ways" were not being sufficiently honored, or that ancestral values were not being treated with the piety they deserve.[2] Charges like these continue to echo through the centuries, but one has to wait until relatively recent times to hear another, very different charge: that *tradition itself* is disappearing, or that it is simply no longer able to provide the thread needed to keep the fabric of social life from unravelling.

A variety of explanations have been given to account for the alleged disintegration of tradition in the modern period. I will discuss these explanations later in the book, but for now it is important to point out that this supposed "withering away" of tradition has provoked two contradictory responses. The first is that the decline of tradition is an unmitigated disaster. Without tradition, it is said, we are thrown into

3

spiritual and moral decay. Life becomes increasingly empty and vac-
uous, as entire populations become unable to discern what is valuable
from what is valueless. Furthermore, without tradition people are said to
lose touch with whole realms of experience and meaning which had
been nourished for generations, but which are now slipping out of reach.
In light of this, a new task is proclaimed for the contemporary age,
namely to hold onto, recover, or restore tradition as much as is humanly
possible, since ultimately the alternative to preservation or restoration is
nihilism.

The second response is that the decline of tradition is emancipatory,
that at bottom tradition is only constraint which stifles originality and
hinders human possibilities. Whereas a Heidegger could argue that
"everything essential and of great magnitude has arisen only out of the
fact that man . . . was rooted in a tradition," this second position pro-
claims that true creativity is released only *after* tradition has been done
away with.[3] Hence the apparent collapse of tradition is celebrated not
only because it opens the way to new forms of artistic and cultural
expression, but also because it makes possible styles of life and modes of
individualism that were unimaginable in traditional societies. For those
who have adopted this point of view, there is no thought of rescuing
tradition from its seemingly desperate situation. Quite the contrary, the
emphasis is on reveling in the new levels of freedom that become
available once the dead weight of the past has been sprung into the air.

Though these two responses illuminate different sides of the problem
of tradition, they nevertheless represent what Hegel in another context
called "two lifeless extremes." In my opinion, neither offers a productive
way of thinking about tradition. I believe what is needed now is a fresh
look at the problem beyond these two perspectives, and that is what I
have sought to achieve in this book.

My position is that the demise of tradition, though real, can easily be
exaggerated. Many traditions continue on in the nooks and crannies of
modern life. They exist privately even where they have eroded publicly.
Some survive by going underground, others by reconstituting themselves in such a way as to live on in new forms and guises. Yet even
granting these exceptions, it is undeniable that numerous traditions
which once flourished are now either in eclipse or have disappeared
altogether. Many of these weakened or lost traditions are only minimally
significant, and consequently their fate has hardly been noticed. But
some of them are "substantive traditions," i.e., long-standing modes of

thought or practice that for centuries have organized social and cultural life in the West.[4] Most of these substantive traditions have now lost their influence. Not only has the general stock of such traditions been depleted, but many of those that have survived appear to be thinner, more anemic, than they were in earlier times. For this reason, the old, substantive traditions have become incapable of providing the glue to bond together social life. Much of the cohesion we now have depends on the substitutes that have replaced the great traditions such as bureaucratic organization, consumer capitalism, and media culture.

It is true that many of the once dominant traditions contained biases and prejudices we would now consider unacceptable. To romanticize tradition often does violence to past suffering by holding up as exemplary much that should be deplored.[5] Yet there are also hidden dangers in the surrogates that now stand in for tradition. Because of the enormous power they wield over all aspects of modern life, the state, the market, and the culture industry exercise perhaps more control over thought and behavior than the traditions ever did. At least throughout much of the past one tradition could be counterposed to another, thereby preventing any from holding absolute sway. Today, however, such a strategy of balance is difficult to achieve, since we have on hand very few defenses against the forces of administration or manipulation that have their source *outside* the old traditions, and that seem bent on destroying what those traditions represent. Though we might appear to be freer than our forebears, we may now actually be more vulnerable to a host of new and more effective political and economic determinations.

In light of the dangers inherent in modernity, one tendency is to want to retreat into an allegedly "better" past. This option, which has been well articulated by various traditionalist movements in this century, cannot be taken seriously as we prepare to enter the twenty-first century. Though there may be something attractive about the idea of retreat, particularly since it contains an implicitly critical attitude (i.e., an attitude based on a refusal of "what is"), it is also fundamentally unrealistic. There can be no literal going back to some earlier point in time once it has been transcended, and by the same token there can be no forced or artificial reconstitution of the past within the present. In my view, the only real choice available to the individual today is to embrace modernity rather than run away from it. Of course, this is the message one hears continually within present-day culture. The prevailing advice in much of the popular media as well as in postmodernist currents of thought is to

5

accept the world as it is, and celebrate with "joyous affirmation" its multitudinous possibilities. But when I suggest that we embrace modernity I mean that we embrace it *critically*. (In this respect, I may be closer in spirit, though not in method, to those who recommend withdrawal.) My contention is that the best way to accept modernity and yet maintain a critical attitude toward it is to *return to tradition*—not, however, in order to stay there, but rather to bring tradition forward in such a manner as to disturb, not affirm, the clichés and complacencies of the present.

Hence, in this book I advocate a return to tradition, but only if done in the right way. This will require a serious rethinking of the standard notions of what tradition is and what it is supposed to do. Such a rethinking is difficult because the concept of "tradition," like the concept of "culture," has always been heavily inflected with conservative meanings and implications. Ideologically speaking, tradition has been used more often to defend an established reality than to oppose it. However, in the following pages I have approached tradition from new angles in order to, as it were, rub tradition against its own grain. Especially in the latter part of the book I suggest a number of ways to critically reappropriate both discontinued and still-surviving traditions. My assumption is that a reappropriation is necessary not only to recover values and meanings in danger of being lost (generally the conservative position), but also to challenge—intellectually and practically—those aspects of the present age that appear most ominous, and which therefore ought not to be passed over in silence.

This work is designed to be exploratory rather than definitive, suggestive rather than comprehensive. Some of the chapters that follow are more theoretical than others, but I have tried throughout to buttress my arguments with pertinent examples and illustrations. My decision to write this book more on the order of a French *essai* than a German monograph is one reason it is shorter and more condensed than it might have been. Another reason for the book's brevity is that, although I sometimes talk about tradition in general, I have mostly confined my discussion to that part of the world I know best, namely the industrialized West (Europe and the United States) in the nineteenth and twentieth centuries.

In Chapter 1, I offer a working definition of the term "tradition." Chapters 2 and 3 provide a brief historical account of the fate of tradition in the West since the early modern period. Chapter 4 deals with the treatment of tradition by both the modern centralized state and the commercial market. Chapter 5 is a theoretical interlude in which I raise a number of issues having to do with the status of tradition at the present time. Some of the questions I pose and attempt to answer here are: Is there such a thing as a human "need for tradition?" If there is, what becomes of this need when traditions actually or apparently disappear? Is it possible that people still require tradition today, but in an entirely different way than they did in the past? Must it be said that tradition is always something stabilizing and integrative, or can it just as well be critical and disruptive? In Chapter 6, I discuss a variety of ways in which traditions which now seem lost might be reappropriated. Chapter 7 focuses on the methods of recovering and refunctioning traditions that have persevered, but in distorted or "inauthentic" forms. Chapter 8 discusses some ways of looking at other traditions that have survived intact, but only by becoming marginalized or socially irrelevant. The book concludes with suggestions concerning how best to think about tradition *within* modernity, and tradition *against* modernity.

1 The Meaning of Tradition

Definitions

The term "tradition" refers to a set of practices, a constellation of beliefs, or a mode of thinking that exists in the present, but was inherited from the past. Many things now in existence were engendered in the present as a response to something present. A tradition, by contrast, requires the prior existence of something else which is then imitated or repeated. Thus, when J.G.A. Pocock defines a tradition as an "indefinite series of repetitions of an action, which on each occasion is performed on the assumption that it had been performed before," he is not quite correct.[1] It is not the assumption that an act was previously performed that makes it traditional; rather, it becomes traditional when it is replicated precisely *because* it was performed before. In every bona fide tradition, there is always an element of the prescriptive.

A tradition, then, can be a set of observances, a collection of doctrines or teachings, a particular type of behavior, a way of thinking about the world or oneself, a way of regarding others or interpreting reality. All of these are examples of traditions when they are active and alive in the present, even though they originated in the past. But other things in the present that come from the past are not traditions. These would include various manmade objects or artifacts from former times, symbols or images passed down through the centuries, or institutions that survive from one generation to the next. All of these may be conduits of traditional attitudes or patterns of conduct, but they are not themselves traditions. An antique artifact might suggest something traditional, by reference or association, but in and of itself it is not a tradition. A symbol from the past could refer to traditional values without being a tradition. A long-standing institution might likewise be a carrier of traditions, but it would be incorrect to call the institution itself a tradition. The Catholic Church, for example, is an institution that preserves certain traditions of practice and belief. But it is the religious practices and beliefs that are the actual traditions; the Church is only the medium through which they are shaped, organized, and carried forward in time.

The literal definition of tradition is worth recalling. The term comes from the Latin verb *tradere* meaning to transmit, to give up, or to give over. *Traditio* indicates the process by which something is transmitted; *traditum* refers to the thing transmitted. (On this basis, the *Oxford English Dictionary* defines tradition as "the act of 'handing down' . . . from one to another, or from generation to generation," and *Webster's Dictionary* describes it as an "act of delivering into the hands of another" or "the handing down of knowledge through successive generations.") Significantly, the root word *tradere* means not only to transmit or to give over, but also to give something to someone for safe-keeping, as in giving one a deposit. This latter meaning is the one that took hold in Roman Jurisprudence, especially with respect to the laws of inheritance. The resonance of this meaning passed over into the term "tradition," and the result is revealing. What is implied by *traditio* is that (*a*) something precious or valuable is (*b*) given to someone in trust after which (*c*) the person who receives the "gift" is expected to keep it intact and un-harmed out of a *sense of obligation* to the giver.

Here it is important to say that the language of Roman Law did not invent, but simply codified, what may be the oldest obligation conceived of by human beings: the obligation to preserve and cherish something which someone (an ancestor, a predecessor) considered valuable enough to pass on, and to do this out of an abiding respect for that individual.[2] The duties that from earliest times were thought to accompany this sacred transmission may be the origin of the concept of responsibility. They might also have served as a primitive source of the concept of guilt. It is possible that the sense of guilt (and remorse) may have initially been felt as disloyalty to ancestors, based on some notion that, as Nietzsche put it, a "pledge [had been] broken." If so, the primordial crime would not have been the killing of the "old man of the horde," as Freud described it in *Totem and Taboo,* but rather some failure to keep intact what was handed down in trust.

In those historical ages in which the central responsibility involved receiving something valuable, preserving it, and then passing it on to those who come after, tradition provided the cohesion that held together

social life. At the same time, by indicating what was culturally normative, tradition established a framework for meaning and purpose: it told
people what they should do in order to be in harmony with the world. No
less important, tradition shaped notions of authority. It made it clear that
the authoritative was always that which was handed down from the past
through the medium of tradition. Practically speaking, tradition was
always authoritative, and authority always traditional.

For any tradition to be authentic, it would seem that at least three
conditions need to be satisfied.[3] First, at the very minimum a tradition
must link together three generations (i.e., two transmissions), though of
course, at the opposite extreme, there is no limit to the time span of a
tradition, since some have obviously lasted for centuries or millennia.
Second, a tradition, in conveying a sense of the past in the present, must
not merely represent something old or ancient, but must also carry a
certain amount of spiritual or moral prestige. Third, a tradition must
convey a sense of continuity between the past and present. By continuity
I mean something different than the simple preservation of an isolated
quantum of the past in the present. A tradition also has to give one a
feeling that it has been sequentially passed down through time, that it
has the force of temporal duration behind it. Then, upon receiving a
tradition, one feels part of something continuous, as if one were a link in
a chain stretching back in time.

Though this feeling of consecutiveness seems to be essential to any
genuine tradition, a couple of qualifications should be made to this
general rule. Sometimes a tradition might appear to be radically discontinuous. It may seem to disappear altogether, only to resurface at a later
date. What often happens in such cases is that the tradition does in fact
maintain its continuity, but underground and out of sight. This occurs
especially with those traditions that are repressed or persecuted by
official society. Even though they may seem to have been abolished, they
actually slip just below the surface and preserve themselves in secrecy,
as happened with many of the medieval heresies. In southern France in
the early thirteenth century, for example, the Catholic Church believed
it had rooted out all traces of the Cathar heresy. By means of crusades
and inquisitions, the Church did indeed appear to have eradicated Cathari religious beliefs, and yet we know now that Cathari traditions
survived in pockets of France and Italy for several more generations—at
least until the middle of the fourteenth century. The doctrinally less

extreme Waldensians were also thought to have been destroyed. Nevertheless, in ways not clear to church or state, their traditions seemed mysteriously to reappear from time to time. The reigning authorities had trouble accounting for the sporadic reemergence of strains of belief that were supposed to have been eliminated. In truth, there was nothing inexplicable about it; Waldensian religious traditions had only vanished from the view of the persecutor, while all the time remaining active at a subterranean level.[4]

The other qualification to the general rule of consecutiveness is that sometimes traditions do literally come to an end—that is to say, they exhaust themselves in one form (say, as a series of practices) but continue on in another (a set of beliefs). Hence, over long periods of time traditional modes of behavior occasionally die out, not just retreat underground. When this happens, such modes of behavior may be converted into sets of ideas or teachings which continue to be handed down and strongly affirmed as values, even where they are not simultaneously embodied in conduct. It is conceivable that after a while, under favorable conditions, a tradition of belief could be reconverted into a tradition of practice similar to the one that had earlier come to an end. This kind of reconversion could occur if there is only an apparent rupture in the tradition, not a real loss of filiation with a past that is still carried forward intellectually or doctrinally, in memory or in key texts preserved over time. It would seem that a number of African traditions survived in this manner among slaves in the American South. So long as they were bound to their masters, most slaves were able to preserve certain traditions only *in thought,* but once set free they were able, if they chose, to transform the memory of previous traditions into the actual *practice* of those traditions. The experience of Orthodox Jews in the U.S.S.R. provides a more recent example of the same process. From the beginning of the Revolution, but especially since the 1930s, official governmental policy called for the assimilation of the divergent peoples of the Soviet Union. The projected goal was the creation of a single "communist identity," in light of which the continued existence of Jewish religious and cultural traditions was viewed as dangerously counterproductive. The result was forced acculturation of the Jews, among others, into Soviet society. Despite numerous restrictive measures including the closing of Orthodox schools and synagogues, Jewish traditions were passed down covertly. Only in the late 1980s, with the abandonment of assimilationist policies, did it become possible for Jews not only to believe in the tenets of their religion, but also to *act on* their beliefs in public ritual and ceremony without direct interference from the state.[5]

Traditions and Customs

From what has been said so far, a tradition might seem barely distinguishable from a custom. A custom is an established social usage that has been built up through repetition over a long period of time. It may originate to satisfy some immediate need, but in the course of being repeated from one generation to another it gradually comes to be accepted simply because it is convenient, or because it has been in operation for so long that no one questions its rationale. In this respect a custom seems to do what a tradition does: it brings the past into the present, preserves a sense of continuity, and endures for a sufficiently long time. How then does a custom differ from a tradition?

Though the lines between the two are easily blurred, there are some notable differences. Customs are social practices which, when considered from the point of view of society as a whole, are judged to be much less important than traditions. Because customs involve mostly superficial modes of behavior, they are not as heavily invested with value as traditions are. For example, the use of Roman numerals today, although we have largely adopted the Arabic system, is a custom; it is simply not important enough to be called a tradition. Certain long-standing modes of greeting, like the Japanese bow or the American handshake, are also customs rather than traditions, since they amount to relatively insignificant social habits. Moreover, customs seldom carry real prescriptive power. Although they are, in effect, culturally recommended patterns of behavior, following them is usually not insisted upon.[6] Customs are often adhered to out of expediency or inertia. Moral censure is rarely incurred if one deviates from them, whereas traditions carry some amount of moral authority. By the same token, customs are by and large passively received and passively handed down. They are acquired almost unconsciously, through "unreflective imitation," whereas traditions are more actively embraced and transmitted because of the greater value attached to them.[7]

Despite these differences, traditions cannot always be sharply distinguished from customs. In some of the patterns and rhythms of everyday life, for example, one can detect not just customs but real traditions.

12

These traditions may not be consciously received or passed on as traditions usually are, but as people reproduce their daily lives they perpetuate certain traditions whether they fully intend to or not. Various ethnic and regional traditions have long been transmitted this way, which is to say, they are carried forward not by design, but as part of the warp and woof of quotidian existence. Likewise, though most traditions (unlike customs) have their own discourses through which they explain what they are and mean, some do not. Some are simply practices that have not been raised to reflexivity, as may be the case with certain kinds of skills handed down only as "know-how." Even if such skills or practices are never formally articulated, they can still be regarded as legitimate traditions and not merely as lowly customs.[8]

Hence, the boundary separating custom from tradition is not always easy to discern. Distinguishing between the two becomes all the more difficult when one realizes that traditions can gradually turn into customs, and vice versa. The conversion of a tradition into a custom takes place when a tradition becomes routinized, or when its moral authority wears down after a long period of transmission.[9] The conversion of a custom into a tradition occurs when a long-established custom is consciously reassessed, and in the process raised to a higher level of importance. This kind of reassessment often happens when people become acutely aware of the traditions and customs of others, due either to conquest or to the spread of knowledge from one culture to another. Occasionally an awareness of alien practices and beliefs causes people to see their own customs in an entirely different light. They may then begin to value their customs as things to be cherished, preserved, and conscientiously passed on to descendants so as not to be lost under the impact of foreign influences.

Tradition and Change

Not only do traditions become customs and customs traditions, but once traditions are established they themselves change in the process of being handed down. Nothing historically engendered ever remains fixed or static. The totality of relations that encompasses a receiving generation is never exactly the same totality that was taken for granted by the transmitting one. As social and cultural changes occur, so do ways of confronting and organizing experience. And as experiences change, so do modes of perception, including perceptions of what a tradition is and means. When needs and perceptions shift, no matter how slightly, the inherited traditions cannot help but be apprehended and assimilated differently. Hence, no tradition is ever taken over precisely as it was given, or passed on precisely as it was received. Rather, it is always *adapted to a situation*. If a situation includes new elements not previously encountered, a tradition is rarely embraced just as it is, but is instead selectively adopted, and thereby modified and altered.[10] Historically speaking, there is always some amount of noncongruence between one generation's definition of "reality" and another's. The greater the changes that occur in the world-as-it-is, or in how that world is organized and interpreted, the greater the degree of noncongruence there will be between generations, and the more necessary it will be to adjust or attune a tradition to the new circumstances.

For example, there are at least three mental outlooks a receiving generation could adopt as a result of pressures from a changing sociocultural reality. Each outlook would help determine how an existing tradition would come to be assimilated and carried forward. If the changes in the world-as-given are very slight from one generation to the next, the tradition might be accepted more or less as it is, with only microscopic emendations. This appears to be what happened during long stretches of prehistory, as well as in stable peasant communities within historical time, when there were very few changes in the basic forms of social life over centuries. If, however, the world changes more significantly, the tradition might have to be thoroughly reworked in order to make it more relevant. This is what occurred in the early modern period when many traditions were preserved and yet revamped to accommodate new social and political realities. And finally, if the world changes drastically in the short time-span between predecessors and successors, then the major tenets of the tradition might encounter large-scale reevaluation or opposition.[11] This is what has taken place during the past two centuries due to wars, economic breakdowns, and political and industrial revolutions. In each instance there is still a *reception* of the tradition, but with varying degrees of enthusiasm or respect for it.

Put differently, if a tradition is a conversation stretching over time,[12] then it is also a conversation that can take a variety of forms extending from the genial to the acrimonious. In the first example mentioned above—where a tradition is accepted without contestation—the conversation is virtually one way: the tradition dictates and the receivers of the tradition listen. In the second example, a more critical attitude emerges:

the tradition is assimilated, but not unthinkingly, since a kind of dialogue with it is opened up wherein both the tradition and the generation that acquires it are on more or less equal footing. And in the last example, where the tradition is more seriously called into question, a conversation of sorts still exists, but it is more confrontational, bordering on the argumentative. In each instance, the conversation with tradition remains, but it is conducted in different ways. As we will see later, there is yet a fourth position possible, which is to break off the conversation altogether. Were this to occur—and in the view of some it has already occurred—there would be no interaction with tradition at all. Whatever "speech" might then emerge would be entirely self-generated, for, with the dialogue with tradition at an end, there would be nothing coming from the past that could provide even the rudiments of a meaningful discourse.

The Medium of Transmission

Other factors besides the shifting configurations of reality cause changes in tradition over time. One of the most important is the means by which a tradition is handed down, for the medium of transmission can materially affect both the content of a tradition and the way it is assimilated by a receiving generation.

When, for instance, a tradition is transmitted orally—as from the old to the young in a small community, or from parents to children in a family—it achieves an immediacy that helps insure faithful repetition, with perhaps only slight variations. Moreover, since the transmitters of word-of-mouth traditions are physically present, they can monitor the reception to make sure that the traditions are properly acquired according to their standards. It may not be surprising, then, that where oral transmission is the rule, traditions are more likely to be picked up as tacit knowledge; they become an integral part of one's "natural attitude" and hence penetrate to a deeper level of social character or personality.

The situation changes considerably when writing is the means of transmitting a tradition. By being encoded in words, traditions get organized, structured, and passed down differently, and this in turn affects their form and content. Although writing makes transmission more precise, it does so at the expense of the immediacy and intimacy that comes with oral tradition. When the receptor of tradition is the eye rather than the ear, a greater emotional distance from the tradition seems to be the rule. The very fact that a tradition can be transcribed into a text alters its character, for as a text, a tradition is more easily scrutinized for discrepancies and contradictions that are not detectable in speech. Where oral transmission is dominant, one works hard enough simply to remember the tradition accurately; there is little room for a critical attitude. But where written transmission prevails, the tradition becomes objectified and consequently is made more accessible to examination and critical reflection. A cooler, more analytical attitude toward tradition becomes possible when it is converted into an "object of visual as well as aural inspection."[13] Hence, whenever a tradition is acquired textually, it tends to be grasped as abstract knowledge rather than as something immediately, palpably present. Although this might help sharpen an understanding of tradition, at the same time it is likely to weaken allegiance to it.

Despite some of the apparent disadvantages of written over oral transmission, writing generally became the preferred mode of transmission because written traditions permitted more exactitude, a feature useful to those in authority. Written traditions were also more easily manipulated, since those encoded in legal statutes, sacred books, and the like were by definition accessible only to the literate, who then claimed to possess an exclusive right to interpret them. By contrast, oral transmission was much more diffuse and idiosyncratic, and consequently not as susceptible to control or management from the top down. Thus, even though the oral mode of handing on tradition came first in time, and was for most of human history the *only* means by which traditions were communicated, it gradually gave way to the written mode of transmission. This of course did not mean that oral traditions disappeared. They continued, and still continue, alongside written traditions, but usually in a position of secondary importance, at least from the point of view of centralized power. What should be kept in mind, then, is that although writing slowly usurped or displaced speech as the main conduit of tradition, it by no means abolished it. Numerous traditions are still conveyed by word of mouth, even though this method is regarded as inferior, more appropriate for minor than for major social traditions.[14]

It should be noted that the same tradition can be handed down through two different channels, an oral and a textual one, with the result that what was originally one tradition can begin to look and feel like two separate traditions. For example, over the centuries in Europe a number of Christian religious traditions which were passed on orally through the medium of popular culture, were simultaneously handed down in writing from one theologian to another within the framework of an elite literary-theological culture. After a long span of time, what was initially the same tradition evolved into two different traditions that seemed to bear only minimal relation to one another. Something similar happened within Jewish religious traditions when the ways parted between rabbinical (textual) and popular (oral and aural) modes of transmission. Wherever splits like these occur, two separate traditions really can evolve, each shaped by its own particular means of transmission. More common, however, is something like a continuous intertwining of the two strains within the same tradition, each strain being only apparently independent of the other. In Christianity, there had been for centuries a constant interaction between popular traditions (usually more emotional, pietistic, and syncretic) on the one hand, and theological ones (usually intellectual, dogmatic, and purist) on the other. Each has always been aware of and in crucial ways affected by the presence of the other. Similarly, in Judaism, the Hasidic movement in Eastern Europe during the eighteenth century and after defined itself against Orthodoxy in order to clarify what it was for. And rabbinical Judaism, in turn, used Hasidism to point out the dangers that lie in wait when people depart from "official" interpretations of Jewish scriptural traditions. In both of these cases, as in many others like them, popular and elite currents within the same traditions continuously intermingled with and influenced each other, sometimes in positive and sometimes in negative ways.[15]

Finally, when the transmission of a tradition is neither exclusively oral nor strictly literary, but institutional, there are still other ways in which a body of tradition can be affected. For one thing, when traditions are institutionalized they begin to be conveyed and received formally, not tacitly. The rules and procedures of transmission become more tightly controlled. Often, an official canon of acceptable traditions emerges which becomes rigid and exclusionary. Likewise, institutionalized traditions tend to become more specialized. In many cases, they are lifted out of the public sphere where they may once have been available to everyone in at least rudimentary form, and are turned over to more narrowly focused academies, conservatories, or seminaries where they are communicated as highly specialized bodies of information, often with degrees and certificates to prove intellectual mastery. The results can sometimes be favorable, especially if the traditions would otherwise

17

wither for lack of support. But traditions can also be distorted through too much institutional interference. Particularly if they are preserved only artificially, they can slip into a kind of Alexandrian aridity where technical knowledge *about* tradition becomes a substitute for tradition itself. Here, too, the mechanics of transmission can leave a mark on both the appearance and the substance of a tradition.

In the life of any tradition, no matter how many changes it undergoes, at least a few persistent elements remain from beginning to end.[16] If they did not persist, the tradition would not be recognizable as the same tradition. However, these elements are sometimes easy to miss because of all the additions, modifications, or embellishments a tradition can take on over the years. After a certain point, the supplementary meanings affixed to a tradition can begin to obscure the often overlooked constants of a tradition. Written traditions are especially susceptible to this process when an excess of commentary, accumulated from one generation to the next, attaches itself to the original tradition and becomes fused with it. This can so overburden the original tradition that its primary meanings may appear to be occluded, even though they continue in some form underneath or within the encumbrances.

This problem is compounded by the fact that a receiving generation may not be able to distinguish a tradition's original elements from its secondary elaborations. Generally speaking, people assimilate a tradition as it is; they do not try to figure out where and when increments were added or alterations made. Consequently, the most archaic residues and most recent additions are usually mixed together in ways likely to confuse earlier participants in the tradition who would be unfamiliar with the new amalgam that is now taken to be the tradition. Only a careful historical study of the tradition would be able to separate the newer from the older elements, or explain when and why the new elements were incorporated or the old ones discarded. To grasp such distinctions, a certain distancing from the tradition would be necessary, for without critical distance, the tradition could not be subjected to serious inquiry. But here, paradoxically, the costs are great, since the more a tradition becomes an object of scrutiny, the less one is able to treat it as a value in its own right. In Chapter 5, I argue in a more focused way for the value of tradition, but not for its *intrinsic* value. In my view, the value of tradition is relative, not absolute. My "defense" of tradition in the second half of this book relates to the context in which we live, a context that seems increasingly traditionless by the standards of the past. If the absence of tradition is indeed the rule today, then tradition's primary importance may lie precisely in its profound difference from, or non-identity with, the present. Before elaborating on this point, I want to explain how we have arrived at our present situation by examining what appears to be a precipitous decline of tradition in the modern period.

2 Tradition under Stress

The Function of Tradition

Human beings have lived together in settled communities for perhaps fifteen thousand years. If a new generation appears roughly every twenty-five years, then communal existence can be said to have lasted for some six hundred generations. What brought people together during this long span of time was the basic collective need to survive; what bound them together culturally and emotionally, however, was the glue of tradition. Tradition defined values, established continuities, and codified patterns of behavior. For the millennia in which tradition ruled unchallenged, the guidelines for life were those concisely summarized by Jeremiah in the Old Testament: "Stand in the [old] ways, and look, and ask for the old paths, where the good is, and walk in it, and find rest for your soul" (Jeremiah, 6:16). Almost all the important elements of a traditional attitude are expressed here: that the old ways are the best; that value is found by following the old paths; that comfort and peace come by holding on to the legacies of the past; and that "the past" and "the good" are for all practical purposes one and the same.

Clearly, during the long expanse of time that preceded the early modern era, tradition was crucial for individual and communal life because it did what nothing else was able to do. It supplied the central categories through which the world could be understood. It provided the order that helped stabilize social existence. It set one right with ancestors whose heritage had to be preserved. It fortified community ties (a community being those who share the same traditions) and gave people a sense of belonging.

In addition to all this, tradition helped foster certain mental dispositions which then served to strengthen tradition's hold on the thought and practice of individuals. For instance, tradition encouraged attitudes of piety and reverence toward what was inherited from the past, attitudes which, in turn, deepened the inherently conservative dispositions of archaic societies. Similarly, tradition produced respect for authority (with the authoritative always understood as the accumulated wisdom of the past), a respect that reinforced the grip of tradition on social life. And finally, tradition helped affirm the notion that one had to look backward toward some distant origin to find the source of all value. Throughout most of the past the assumption was that value itself was created by supernatural beings at some remote point in time: the so-called time of the "beginnings." Once value was created, however, it became the font of all meaning. The key, then, was to get back in touch with the primordial time of the beginnings and draw on its power for renewal in the present. One way to achieve this was through sacred rituals or ceremonies of reenactment that made symbolic contact with the origins. Another way was through the medium of tradition, for tradition was understood to be a continuous temporal chain linking the present to the most distant past. By following tradition backward from an impoverished "now" to a rich and plentiful "then," one could gain access to the time of creation. Hence it was essential to preserve tradition, since it supplied a direct, sequential link to the original source of value. Without this connection, the world ran the risk of being cut off from meaning.[1]

Breakdown

Many other factors sustained tradition over the long duration of human history. In the West, from the time of the earliest Near Eastern civilizations up until the late Middle Ages, mythical and religious systems helped buttress traditional world views; so did powerful political institutions, communal associations, and the inertia of everyday life. Yet despite these forces, tradition as social cement gradually lost a good deal of its integrative power. The internal reason for this loss had to do with the problems of transmitting tradition; the external reason lay in the emergence of new modes of thought which served to undermine the effectiveness of tradition.

With regard to the first reason, as social life became more highly differentiated, it became obvious that there were not just one or two unifying traditions, but a multitude of different traditions operating simultaneously in different spheres. This had not been the case in the very earliest tribal communities or primitive settlements. At that point, all the important traditions were known and shared by the entire group, since there was as yet no complex division of labor, no written tradition to compete with an oral one, and only minimal contact with strangers who might represent different ways of thinking. With the passage of time, however, these communities evolved into more intricate social systems. In part, this happened as a response to a changing external environment, but it was also due to a variety of internal pressures which necessitated the creation of new social tasks, new roles, and new sets of relationships within the collectivity itself. The result of such developments was not a "weakening" of tradition in the strict sense of the word, for tradition remained the primary force holding together primitive societies. Rather, the result was a fragmentation and dispersal of tradition. For along with the expansion of social roles and functions came new spheres of life, each with its own set of traditions which sometimes competed with those simpler but more unifying traditions that had once been unchallenged. Though the most important religious and cultural traditions continued to be adhered to by all members of the earliest societies, many narrower and more localized "little traditions" also took hold, expanded, and proliferated.[2] If one looks only at the West from the time of the first small communities, through the period of the ancient civilizations, up to the Middle Ages, one sees that these more focused traditions eventually grew into full-fledged class, occupational, and regional traditions. They became clearly demarcated rural and urban traditions, court and guild traditions, aristocratic and peasant traditions, learned and popular traditions, and so on. With this kind of differentiation, it obviously became impossible for all members of society to share all the traditions. Instead, each individual assimilated only a small portion of the traditions current during his or her lifetime. The rest were either not noticed at all (since they were too distant from one's daily experience), or if noticed, disregarded (because they were judged to be inappropriate for one's station in life). At the same time, different people tended to embrace even the same traditions with different degrees of intensity. For some, a tradition might be something to imitate exactly, rigorously, conscientiously. For others it might be no more than a rough guideline for action or belief, with plenty of room for deviation. In any case, wherever the amount of allegiance to be given to tradition became a matter of choice, the authority of tradition itself was diminished, and its hold on people was consequently lessened.

As traditions became more specialized, they also became more vulnerable to numerous internal strains. New tensions appeared not just between the all-embracing and the little traditions, but also within each tradition. This development led to competing interpretations of the same tradition, and eventually to the emergence of rival traditions. Once rival traditions appeared, people became freer to select the traditions they wanted, even to the point of leaving one tradition and attaching themselves to another. One result of this process was that tradition in general became less prescriptive. Eventually many of the traditions that continued to be handed down were transmitted more carelessly and indifferently, since there was less communal pressure to support and reinforce the value of tradition itself. Again, to confine the discussion to the West, something like this voluntary adherence to tradition and the accompanying looseness of transmission seems to have occurred by the early modern period (roughly the fifteenth to the seventeenth centuries), with the result that many once-important traditions slowly began to lose their cohesive force. At about the same time, a print culture began to replace an oral culture in many parts of Europe and the New World. This meant that some key traditions came to be passed down—if they were passed down at all—more as texts than as practices. As already mentioned, though writing preserves tradition more exactly, it also makes it easier for people to regard their traditions merely as ideas rather than imperatives. This, too, helped emotionally distance many people from tradition, thereby significantly reducing its sway over social life.

Empiricism and Rationalism

Along with these internal reasons for the slackening of tradition were external reasons set in motion by the social and economic forces unleashed by the breakup of the medieval world. Accompanying the societal changes were new ways of thinking which challenged older, more traditional modes of thought. But it was neither the Renaissance nor the Reformation, as some have supposed, that fundamentally altered the primacy of tradition, for both of these movements were in their own ways backward-looking. Though both defined themselves against *some* traditions, they were even more firmly set upon restoring others, with the result that neither can be said to have undermined the importance of tradition as such.[3] Rather, the most serious early challenge to tradition came from other intellectual developments underway around the same time, and it was these that more radically subverted the certainties of the traditional outlook. For our purposes, only three of these developments need to be mentioned here.

The first development was empiricism, or the notion that only what can be directly confirmed by observation and sense experience can be true. When a notion such as this appears, tradition cannot help but be undermined, for the truth claims of tradition are invariably deductive not inductive, dogmatic not empirical. Francis Bacon was one among many who opened the door to this new manner of thinking. For him, the goal of an individual should be to approach the world exactly as it is given to the senses, and thus without any reliance on received ideas. But all traditions are by definition received ideas. Wherever traditions exist, there by necessity are "insidious preconceptions" from the past, each one preventing a clear, unbiased perception of the world as it really is. According to Bacon, if life is to be apprehended freshly, the hold of tradition on the human mind had to be broken. Perhaps more than anyone before him, he was consumed with the idea that life is teeming with new and exciting possibilities waiting to be discovered. If the human mind could free itself from the grip of the past, it could not only discover a wealth of new things about the external world, but it could also do something literally godlike: it could *originate,* it could produce ideas never before thought, and create things never previously imagined. In Bacon's view, there was no limit to humanity's capacity for creative generation once a stance of "empirical openness" toward life was adopted.[4]

Despite Bacon's stress on the new and innovative, he was not willing to deny the value of tradition altogether. What he explicitly questioned was only the *truth value* of tradition, not its general usefulness if it could be reformulated in such a way as to produce new understandings.[5] For this to happen, however, tradition would have to become entirely subordinate to sense experience rather than the other way around. More important, it would have to be given the role (which, in his view, was the most useful one it could have) of preparing people for modernity. Bacon was convinced that the "new" was coming whether one liked it or not, so the only issue was whether it would make its appearance disruptively or smoothly. If recombined elements of tradition could be utilized to ease the transition to modern life by putting people in the "right disposition" to accept change, then these elements should not be rejected out of hand. Hence, for Bacon, traditional concepts and images were still valuable, but only to the extent that they helped individuals adjust to the alleged advances of modernity, of which he wholeheartedly approved.[6]

Another new mode of thought, namely rationalism, also emerged around 1600 as an alternative to the traditional outlook. Its sometimes abstract methodologies notwithstanding, the crux of rationalism lay in the simple proposition that the things we can know with the greatest certainty are discoverable not through sense experience, but through the exercise of reason. Though the origins of this point of view go back to Greek philosophy, the claims that began to be made for rationalism became much more assertive by the seventeenth century. These claims proposed that reason is the most credible approach to truth because it is presuppositionless: it posits its own foundations and provides its own criteria for analysis, and therefore requires nothing antecedent to validate itself. Since it is not dependent on experience or history or anything handed down from the past, reason has no need for tradition, which can only hinder the free play of rational thought. Consequently, in place of the authority of tradition, rationalism touted reason as the single most reliable authority and guide not only to life, but to truth as well.

The philosophy of Descartes embodied these new rationalist assumptions. Descartes placed his confidence in the operations of the rational mind unencumbered by the dead hand of the past. According to him, traditions, when closely analyzed, amounted to nothing but a chaos of customs and unverified opinions which mostly fail the test of reason. In the main, traditions seemed to Descartes to perpetuate the "errors" of the past which "make us less capable of correct reasoning."[7] Though Descartes no less than Bacon believed that traditions lead one astray, he did not make their destruction his primary goal. Instead, he treated traditions more as annoyances than formidable adversaries. There are even places in Descartes' work in which he indicates that if elements of tradition could be incorporated into a rational framework, he would not object to their continued existence. "As far as the [traditional] opinions which I had been receiving since my birth were concerned, I could not do better than to reject them completely . . . and [then] *resume them afterwards* . . . when I had determined how they *fit into a rational scheme.* I firmly believed that by this means I would succeed in conducting my life much better than if I built only upon the old foundations [of tradition and custom] . . . without ever having examined them to see if they were true or not."[8]

The Idea of Beginning Again

Finally, a third new mode of thought appeared along with empiricism and rationalism. This one focused on reevaluating the concept of beginnings. As already noted, in a traditional world view, nothing like a "new beginning" was believed possible.[9] There could only be one origin, a single point from which everything else followed. Whatever value or meaning there was in the world was there implicitly at the start and needed only to be unfolded in order to become manifest. The only instances of new beginnings in the Judeo-Christian religious tradition (Noah after the flood, the Incarnation of Christ) were inaugurated by God not man, and even these were not radically new departures, since both were tied to antecedent events. Likewise, in secular history it was inconceivable that there could be, for example, a *re*founding of Rome. Even at critical junctures in their history, the Romans never imagined that they could abolish what the founding of Rome had begun by somehow creating from nothing a *novus ordo saeclorum*. Rather, the goal was at most to restore contact with the origins—i.e., to reinvigorate political life by recalling the beginnings—but never to try and start all over again with some new act of foundation.[10] Attitudes such as these, which effectively sacralized the origins of practically everything important, helped perpetuate traditional patterns of thought for centuries.

In the seventeenth century, however, the idea that it was possible literally to "begin again" was seriously entertained for the first time. Moreover, it came to be assumed that if a second beginning occurred, it could actually be superior to the first one if it managed to wipe away the shortcomings of the original. The notion that something which "follows after" could surpass something that "comes before" was itself virtually without precedent. Conceptually speaking, this idea shattered nearly everything that was taken for granted in the Western intellectual tradition from the time of Homer to the Renaissance. Even Machiavelli, despite his great originality, could not have imagined anything like an authentic second beginning which would supersede and nullify the first. Writing in the early sixteenth century, he still worked within the traditional framework that stressed renewal or restoration, not starting over afresh. "The way to renew [political institutions]," he wrote, "is to carry them back to their beginnings; because all beginnings . . . must possess some goodness by means of which they gain their first reputation and their first growth."[11] In contrast to this notion, the concept of a new beginning meant inaugurating something that never existed before. It meant not completing the past but initiating something wholly separate and distinct from it, and hence privileging (at least implicitly) the present over the past, and the immediate over the transmitted.[12]

One can find the idea that radically new beginnings are possible in the works of thinkers like Bacon and Descartes,[13] as well as in the writings of their followers and intellectual heirs. The notion also appears in the social contract theorists of the seventeenth century. According to these theorists, a social contract represented a legitimate second beginning, in the sense that it abruptly ended one state of affairs (the state of nature) and ushered in an entirely new and different one (a consensual political order). The social covenant Hobbes described, for example, was designed to convert, by means of a single contractual act, an essentially barbaric world into an authentic human community.[14] Hobbes's German contemporary, Samuel Pufendorf, was equally certain that the "social pact" introduced a totally new starting point in history. As he viewed it, whenever a multitude of disparate individuals join together in a covenant to produce "one Compound Person," something wholly without precedent happens. Not only do these individuals pass irreversibly from a natural into a civil state, but just as important, they leave behind their bestial status (*status bestialitatis*) in order to acquire a fully human one (*status humanitatis*).[15] In developing theories such as these, people like Hobbes, Pufendorf, and others took it for granted that, first, there *can* be a starting over from scratch which produces something better than what preceded it; and second, that starting over can be initiated not just by God, but by human beings exercising their own volition. Wherever the possibility of beginning again is present, it would appear that the hold of tradition is weakened, simply because starting over offers a new option. Whereas before only one choice seemed available—that of working within the framework of tradition by "superinducing and engrafting new things upon old" (Bacon)—now another possibility opened up: that of entirely letting go of the past and starting all over again.

Interestingly, once the concept of beginning anew was adopted in the seventeenth century, it came to be thought of both in a temporal and a spatial sense. That is, starting over began to be seen as something that can occur not only at a certain point in time, as with the social contract theorists, but also as a result of a certain way of occupying space. Within this spatial mode, there were two ways of beginning again: one was to leave one physical setting in order to occupy a completely different and hitherto empty space; the other was to enter a space already occupied, clear it out, and then establish a new presence there. The New World exemplified the first type of beginning again, for the European imagination saw America as a virgin land: wild, natural, and for all intents and purposes uninhabited (the Indians seemed not to count). To settle in the New World was viewed as starting afresh in wholly unfamiliar surroundings unencumbered by the past.

Despite the appeal of this notion, the second way of thinking about beginning again appears to have been more pervasive, which only indicates how difficult it was to conceptualize the idea of starting over *ex nihilo*. Not surprisingly, in this second way of thinking, metaphors of building and construction predominated (e.g., razing old structures, clearing away debris, laying new foundations on old sites, etc.). The great legacies of the past were compared to unwieldy edifices that were "badly put together and built up." The old traditions were no more than "magnificent structure[s] without any foundation," and the goal should be not to restore them but to "try the whole thing anew upon a better plan."[16] Even here, however, tradition was not explicitly the enemy. The focus was on carefully cultivating the new in order to *authorize the present* in an entirely different way than it had been authorized in the past—namely, on the basis of its novelty and originality, not on its legacies and inheritances. Thus, when tradition was attacked by seventeenth-century thinkers, it was not so much because they thought of it as an implacable foe; it was simply that tradition seemed to have become an obstacle to this central, authorizing project.

Early Capitalism

Another factor that helped weaken tradition was the emergence of modern capitalism. Though its roots go back to the early Middle Ages and in fact to the ancient world itself, capitalism did not become a major transformative presence in the West until the sixteenth and seventeenth centuries. Once ascendant, however, it promoted a number of values and practices that loosened the hold of tradition on daily life. Because capitalism was not simply an intellectual movement but rather a powerful economic process, it cut much more deeply into the fabric of life than did, say, the ideas of Bacon or Descartes. As a result, capitalism profoundly affected, even revolutionized, virtually every facet of social existence—and almost always in a manner detrimental to tradition.

28

If Max Weber, Werner Sombart, and other scholars of sixteenth-century economic history are correct,[17] early capitalism brought with it a new type of individual. The values and modes of conduct of this new type, the nascent bourgeois, were allegedly different from those that prevailed in traditional cultures. According to Weber, the emergent capitalist individual exhibited the following traits: (1) a tendency to treat objects and persons as means to an end rather than ends in themselves; (2) an inclination to evaluate all undertakings according to the degree of their productiveness; (3) a general orientation to the consequences of actions, not to their historicity (i.e., to how venerable they are, or how firmly they are grounded in past legitimations); (4) a concern that economic activity be guided by rational calculation; and (5) a proclivity for reorganizing everything at hand, including all that is passed down by means of tradition, in order to place it in the service of a new goal: the maximization of profit.

Weber summarized all these traits under the term "*zweckrational* (purposive-rational) behavior." He claimed, on the whole correctly, that these characteristics were emerging particularly among the European middle classes around 1600—though he may have exaggerated the extent to which they were produced or encouraged by the religious doctrines of Calvinism.[18] However that may be, early capitalism did represent, as Weber realized, an emancipation from tradition. This was true both in the goals capitalism advanced (acquisitiveness for its own sake, capital accumulation) and in the methods it provided for achieving them (rational, goal-directed behavior). Old ways of conducting a life based on traditional obligations, duties, and reverences became essentially irrelevant, or at least were relegated to secondary importance. Replacing them was the new capitalist ideal of self-interest, which soon became the pivot around which decisions were made and the value of actions assessed.

The notion that one should follow one's own interests—or even that there was such a thing as a "self" that could define its interests entirely apart from the surrounding community or the legacy of historical traditions—was a relatively new idea in the seventeenth century. The very concept of interests was not central to earlier traditional cultures. Where the term was used at all, it generally carried either a strictly political meaning, as with interest of state, or a narrowly financial one, as in usurious interest.[19] When, in early capitalism, the word interest, or self-interest, began to designate a whole way of life, the term specifically

29

came to mean (*a*) following one's economic advantage, (*b*) on the basis of rational calculation, (*c*) in pursuit of capital accumulation. Wherever rational self-interest was adopted as a mode of being, in the economic sphere or any other, tradition was necessarily impaired. Long-established motives and incentives tended to be slighted, and traditional ways of doing things lost their legitimacy. If following a tradition yielded no practical utility, there was no reason to continue adhering to it simply because it was there. To be sure, the thoroughness of early capitalism's assault on tradition can be exaggerated, for there are many indications that the seventeenth-century businessman carried with him more traditionally patterned modes of behavior than Weber had acknowledged.[20] Nevertheless, it remains true that the middle class in general was a powerful social carrier of early notions of rational behavior and the rational attitude toward life. More than any other class, it inscribed rationality into its daily occupational practices as well as into its styles of self-organization. Thanks primarily to the bourgeoisie, rationalism did not remain simply an intellectual movement limited to the thought of Descartes, Gassendi, and others. Rather, it became something that existed in active, practical form within increasingly large sectors of the middle class from the seventeenth century onward.

The Absolutist State

If capitalism represented an economic challenge to tradition, the rise of the absolutist state in the seventeenth and eighteenth centuries represented a political one. As Gianfranco Poggi has pointed out, the European state passed through several stages from the Middle Ages to 1800.[21] With some exceptions, the typology of development was as follows. First there was the medieval *feudal state,* which was created to address the needs of a basically agrarian, decentralized society. This early state evolved into the *Ständestaat* which predominated from the High Middle Ages to the beginning of the modern period. In the *Ständestaat,* sovereignty was shared between a monarch and a number of representative bodies or estates which spoke mainly for the interests of the nobility and the rising towns. In time, the *Ständestaat* gave way to the *absolutist state* of the late sixteenth through eighteenth centuries. Accompanying this third type of state was a new focus on centralization, an undermining of the earlier division of power between crown and estates, and a completely new agenda of duties and responsibilities which the state took

30

upon itself in order, as it claimed, to better serve the nation. Finally, in the eighteenth and nineteenth centuries in many European countries, the absolutist state gave way to the modern *constitutional state* based on law and the consent of the governed.

On the basis of this rough framework it is possible to argue that the first two types of states supported and deepened many traditional patterns of life, but that, with the ascendancy of the absolutist state systems in the early modern period, numerous traditional values and orientations began to be disrupted. Essentially, there were two processes that came to the fore in conjunction with the rise of the absolutist state, and both proved detrimental to previously established institutions, as well as to the traditional practices those institutions protected.

The first process was the centralization of governmental functions to a more thorough degree than at any earlier time in European history. Many independent assemblies, diets, estates, and corporate bodies, which had long maintained a certain autonomy within the *Ständestaat,* were now allowed to fall into disuse. These various bodies and estates carried with them numerous political traditions that had evolved over the centuries, but when the institutions that housed these traditions were left to decay, the traditions themselves decayed along with them. Where traditions were not weakened as a result of neglect, they were either intentionally pushed into obsolescence, or shrewdly absorbed into a centralized state bureaucracy. The fate of the French *parlements* under Louis XIV provides an example of the first approach. As the French state extended its power, it created its own courts, which in time began to replace the judicial authority of the *parlements,* i.e., the traditional courts that had long been independent of royal control. At first the new state courts of justice were introduced as "exceptions" to the rule, but eventually they themselves became the rule. Of course, this kind of displacement directly served the interests of absolutism, for as royal courts gained leverage over traditional ones, statist conceptions of law were gradually substituted for the old customary laws on which the *parlements* depended.[22]

An example of the second approach mentioned above—that is, the tendency to absorb what could not be pushed aside—is also evident in seventeenth-century France. During the reign of Louis XIV, many traditional representative bodies were superficially preserved, but their functions were redirected to fit the needs of hierarchical state structures. One result of this process was that segments of the old elites which had

31

once been attached to these bodies were stripped of their institutional base and integrated into the enlarged bureaucracy as a service nobility. As these individuals came to identify more and more with the state and its interests, they separated themselves from the traditions they had formerly defended *against* the state. In the meantime, those who resisted being integrated in this manner were simply replaced by a new corps of professionally trained functionaries loyal to the state instead of to local or corporate constituencies.[23]

Also characteristic of the absolutist system in Europe—to stay within the theme of centralization—was the increasing size and authority of the state. As states grew in power, so did their monopoly over the means of coercion, followed by a tightening of the internal mechanisms of social and political control. Wherever absolutist states established themselves, they brought with them an urge to police and regulate. The reasons given for demanding more control were invariably the same: to insure domestic order, to create a more effective administration, or to make the gathering of taxes easier. But always the effect was a greater penetration and disturbance of traditional forms of social life—in fact, a greater "politicization of civil society" (*Verstaatlichung der Gesellschaft*)—than anything seen before. By the seventeenth and eighteenth centuries, the absolutist states stretching from Spain to Russia were claiming jurisdiction over larger and larger areas of life within their domains, including areas that had formerly been governed, if at all, by religious authority or by time-honored but uncodified conventions and traditions.

The absolutist state was driven to regulate not just for the sake of regulation itself, but in order to produce as many uniformities as possible. Uniformity, however, could be achieved only through centralization and bureaucratization, and these processes could only be promoted if the state became more interventionist. It no longer seemed sufficient for the state to be merely defensive vis-à-vis other powerful institutions such as the church. Rather, the emergent absolutist state felt compelled to go on the offensive, to be more purposeful, aggressive, and dynamic, even to the extent of actively supervising many aspects of social and political life which in earlier times it had left alone.[24] Prussia provides perhaps the best example of this development, for there the penetration of the absolutist state into everyday life was more thorough than anywhere else in Europe, France included. What emerged by the eighteenth century in Prussia was an efficient, "well-ordered" policing and regulating state which issued rules and ordinances intended to bring virtually all public (and some private) areas of life under state supervision. The goal of the Prussian state was not just civil *Ordnung*. It was to activate and mobilize the population, to shape and discipline it, in order to draw people out of their traditional indolence and make them more productive for the greater good of the state. This self-given task naturally led to a much greater degree of interference in the society and economy than was true elsewhere. The result was that old group solidarities and practices—now labeled "irrational," or even portrayed as a danger to public health and safety (always an important consideration in the Prussian codes)—were purposely disrupted in an effort to reorganize, regulate, and control them. Naturally, there was some local resistance to governmental encroachment, but the net effect of Prussian policy was, as one historian put it, "to undermine, constrict, and eventually to eliminate what may be called traditional (premodern) patterns of social behavior."[25]

Prussia may represent an exceptional case for the eighteenth century, but it serves as a reminder that when the ideology of *dirigisme* became the rule within the absolutist states, it replaced the rudimentary checks and balances approach of the previous *Ständestaat*. The result was that the old estates and assemblies, many of them institutional carriers of venerable traditions, soon came to be regarded as obstacles to progress or national greatness (both terms defined, of course, by the state). Consequently, these institutions were attacked, subverted, or co-opted, and the traditional values they contained were seriously undermined. Wherever the absolutist state made its appearance, it tried to convince its subjects—and this was the thrust of its centralizing, administrative activity—that *it* was the only legitimate authority, and that all intermediary bodies between the sovereign state and the individual had little legitimacy unless that legitimacy was sanctioned, if not conferred, by the state itself. This led to something that would have been unthinkable earlier: long-standing institutions had either to submit to the state or risk dissolution by state authorities. Even though many *corps intermediares*, including numerous public and private guilds and corporations, were antecedent to the state, they had to be officially registered and chartered by various governmental agencies in order to have even the legal right to continue to exist.[26]

The second process that was speeded up by the absolutist state, in addition to the drive to centralize and regulate, was the rationalization of governmental procedures. This, too, proved harmful to tradition. As the state centralized and standardized its operations, it shifted from what

33

Weber called traditional to rational forms of authority.[27] In doing so, the state became a vehicle for the advancement of political rationalization in the same way that capitalism had become a vehicle for economic rationalization.

Where traditional authority existed, as in both the feudal state and the *Ständestaat,* power was patriarchal. Political legitimacy was based on historical precedent or hereditary connection, and the "sacredness" of what was handed down from the past was rarely questioned. Furthermore, a state founded on traditional authority was not likely to be hostile to the existence of numerous traditional institutions, particularly since they tended to foster a collective, traditionalist cast of mind advantageous to a tradition-minded state. But when rational authority began to replace traditional authority (as in the absolutist state), it stressed the centrality of legal procedures over patriarchy and tradition. Its effectiveness lay in the abstract, formal, and uniform rules that everyone was expected to obey, not only because the rules were rationally formulated, but because they were impersonal and therefore presumably just. Where rational authority held sway there was no need to accentuate the value of custom, precedent, or collective memory, all of which became more or less irrelevant. Only the rationality of the regulations themselves became important.

Later, in the constitutional states of the late eighteenth and nineteenth centuries, these rationalizing tendencies became still more prominent. It does not matter that the constitutional state became more democratic in the process of drawing upon a broader base of popular support. The fact is that even after democratization, states became ever-larger bureaucratic machines. Their procedures became more routinized, and their grounding in purely rational methods of administration more complete. In Chapter 3, more will be said about these processes, but for the time being it is important to note this general rule: that the two principal characteristics of the European absolutist state, the stress on centralization on the one hand and rationalization on the other, helped undermine tradition as a whole—though of course the extent to which this happened varied from one country to another.

The Enlightenment

The Enlightenment of the eighteenth century, particularly as it took shape in France, was the first uncompromisingly antitraditional movement in modern Europe. Moreover, its antitraditionalism was explicit, and not, as with other intellectual movements like empiricism or rationalism, merely implicit. It showed more active hostility, more outright combativeness, toward everything it labeled traditional than any movement that preceded it. The philosophes, as spokesmen at least for the French Enlightenment, were particularly clear that tradition was still a formidable presence in the eighteenth century, especially as it was embodied in institutions like the Catholic Church, in peasant folkways, or in aristocratic structures of power. The sense that their age was potentially a progressive one, even though freighted with residues from the past, was what gave the philosophes one of their central projects in life, namely to eradicate all vestiges of tradition in order to prepare the way for general "social betterment."

Especially for the Enlightenment, several things about tradition made it seem like a negative force. One was the way it allegedly perpetuated prejudices, superstitions, and errors from one generation to the next; another was the way it appeared to hinder human creativity. To the philosophes these two points were inextricably linked. In fact, the first seemed to them the cause of the second, for wherever tradition ruled, the human spirit appeared to be crushed by the dead weight of the past. Because tradition was by its very nature an obstacle to a happier future, it could not simply be dismissed or sidestepped. Nor could it be utilized progressively, as Bacon had hoped, or integrated into a rational framework, as Descartes believed possible. Rather tradition had to be dissolved altogether, for only in this way could a world of light replace a world of darkness.

In addition to these reasons for attacking tradition, the Enlightenment offered others. It argued, for example, that the authority of tradition was based on a false premise which assumed that there was some inherent value in repeating what had gone before. But for the philosophes, the fact that something had previously been thought or done was no reason to repeat it. Only what was judged to be rational carried validity, not what could claim a long line of precedents. As Locke, one of the intellectual heroes of the French Enlightenment, wrote, "[An] argument from what has been to what should of right be has no great force."[28] The philosophes fully concurred. For them, "what has been," meaning particularly the traditions of the past, should not be taken as normative, but rather treated as a burden to be dispensed with as quickly as possible. In his essay "What is Enlightenment?" (1784), Kant expressed a similar view. "Enlightenment," he wrote, "is man's emergence from his self-imposed minority." Wherever the past rules, mankind as a whole is prevented from becoming "mature." The result, according to Kant, is that human beings lose their autonomy and fail to develop according to their highest capacities. His solution to this problem was typical of the Enlightenment's: people must learn to rely on their own understanding and their reason, not on what is handed down on authority, including the authority of tradition. The modern age must "have the courage to use [its] own intelligence." For Kant this meant that it had to begin to trust itself, ask its own questions, and determine its own directions into the future, not merely carry out agendas dictated by the past.[29]

The reasons just mentioned for opposing tradition were more or less abstractly formulated, but the Enlightenment also had other, more concrete, reasons to be against tradition. In France, for instance, the philosophes did not fail to notice that the idea of tradition was frequently put to use ideologically by a resurgent aristocracy eager to reclaim some of the status it had lost during the heyday of absolutism. For this class at the top of society, a defense of tradition specifically meant a defense of hereditary rule, hierarchical relations, and customary rights and privileges. The philosophes valued none of these things. In fact, because they associated themselves with an essentially middle-class world view, they suspected that aristocratic notions of tradition were actually disguises for class rule. Hence, by discrediting what the aristocracy extolled as the "beauty" and "sacredness" of tradition, the philosophes shrewdly found an ideological way to attack the aristocracy, at a time when it was still politically unwise to attack them too vigorously. Similarly, the philosophes noted that at the bottom of French society, among the masses of peasants, tradition was even more powerfully present than at the top. This observation also served their purposes, for the philosophes viewed the woeful state of the rural population as confirmation that where tradition rules, narrowness, ignorance, and provincialism are the result. Either way, whether tradition was identified with the nobility or the peasantry, it represented backwardness to the philosophes. Only by dispensing with it altogether could the way be cleared for real social progress.[30]

Finally, aside from all these arguments, the one case the philosophes pressed most strongly against tradition in any and all of its forms was the notion that it prevented people from being happy. From an Enlightenment perspective, *bonheur* was the true purpose and end of life, but to the philosophes, happiness required freedom.[31] Unless people had the latitude to make choices, exercise judgment, and decide on their own course of action, happiness would forever elude them. But, so the argument went, tradition by its very nature limited freedom. Wherever it became entrenched, it shackled people to dull, rigid, and routinized modes of behavior which produced not pleasure but only stupidity and "insipidness."[32] It followed, therefore, that the cake of custom and tradition had to be broken if people were ever to have a chance to discover happiness. Whereas in earlier times it had been assumed that what happiness there was came from involvement with tradition, now the opposite point of view was offered: that happiness could become a reality only *after* tradition had been abolished.

The Industrial Revolution

The Industrial Revolution began in England in the mid-eighteenth century, and took hold in the rest of Europe and in America during the nineteenth century. Initially it got underway within a traditional social framework, and was even nurtured by some aspects of that framework. Yet, once industrialism acquired a momentum of its own, it reacted back upon and helped undermine the very context that originally produced it.

Despite the various attacks on tradition already mentioned, many social and cultural traditions survived into the eighteenth and nineteenth centuries, mainly because they were rooted in communities that remained intact. Up until the beginning of the Industrial Revolution, the quality and tenor of daily existence for perhaps a majority of people in the West remained relatively stable. Traditions may have been weakened by capitalism, the state, or intellectual movements, but many of them continued to operate effectively at a microlevel. The Industrial Revolution, however, set in motion processes which permanently altered social reality. And when social reality changed, so did the relevance of tradition, since the old ways of doing things no longer seemed to offer viable guidelines for life. For example, one facet of the Industrial Revolution involved a transformation of work in the countryside. When it became clear, thanks to the rapid advances in transportation, that larger profits could be made by producing for European-wide markets instead of small local ones, landowners strove to increase the quantity and quality of their agricultural yields. The easiest and least expensive way of doing this was to modernize production by replacing human and

37

animal power with machine power. The consequence was a gradual mechanization of farming during the nineteenth century, which required an ever-smaller percentage of the population to actually work the land. Those who could no longer make a living in the country found it necessary to leave their rural surroundings. When they did so, they left behind the traditional folkways that had held together social life for generations.

Historians have documented just how extensive this so-called flight from the land was in nineteenth-century industrial Europe.[33] Many of those who departed (perhaps, all told, over thirty million people between the 1830s and World War I) migrated overseas, and hence abandoned their traditional *habitus* altogether.[34] Others, responding less drastically, moved to nearby cities where another facet of the Industrial Revolution, namely the emergence of the factory system, provided employment to former peasants who were transformed into industrial laborers. Either way—whether people were pushed out of the countryside or drawn to the expanding metropolis (or to new lives in foreign lands)—the effect was the same. There was a general uprooting from traditional settings, a separation from old social habits and customs, a loss of communal solidarities. Especially in the burgeoning cities where people became available for completely new modes of social organization, many certainly felt confused and disoriented. And to make matters worse, the churches, which had earlier been the mainstay of rural values, were a generation late in moving to urban areas to address the needs of an emerging industrial working class.[35] In the midst of this value vacuum, and cut off from the security of their former communities, many people found that in order simply to cope with the new routines of daily existence, it made good sense to adapt themselves to nontraditional ideas and ways of life.

This, of course, did not mean that old traditions instantly disappeared. Among the millions who left the countryside either for the industrial city or to settle abroad, many tried to reestablish their rural traditions in urban or foreign settings. Through neighborhood, religious, and ethnic associations, some did manage to maintain ties to the traditional cultural world they had left behind.[36] Nonetheless, the general rule was that industrialism induced people to let go of tradition in the interest of new constructions. Though some old traditions remained intact, many more vanished or were enfeebled once it became evident that industrial modernization had made most of them functionally obsolete.

Of all the antitraditional forces at work between the seventeenth and nineteenth centuries, the Industrial Revolution was surely the most disruptive because it penetrated most deeply into the tissue of everyday life. What it substantially affected was the "lifeworld" (*Lebenswelt*) that had long held together the body of collective experience in the West. The term "lifeworld" refers to the primary reality of daily existence, including the common fund of knowledge which everyone shares, the signs, symbols, and meanings familiar to all, the routines and "stock of interpretive patterns" that are taken for granted as normal.[37] A lifeworld is therefore the frame or background against which a multitude of everyday problems are located and answered. When a lifeworld is firmly in place, everything seems to make sense: the world appears natural, continuous, and comprehensible. With the coming of the Industrial Revolution, however, the lifeworld was disrupted more severely than ever before. At every level of society, old values and assumptions began to weaken under the impact of an expanding industrial economy. And as market incentives gradually came to replace traditional ones, entirely new wants and expectations began to make their appearance.

The more the effects of the Industrial Revolution took hold and eroded older communal contexts and social bonds, the more rapidly the West entered what might be called the epoch of modernity. In the next chapter I will discuss the configurations of this epoch in more detail and describe modernity's impact on tradition in the nineteenth and twentieth centuries.

3 Shaking the Foundations

Modernity

By the middle of the nineteenth century, a number of seemingly modern, as opposed to traditional, assumptions began to be embraced by large segments of the Western world. Before turning to the results of this development, I want briefly to summarize what historians take to be some of the main characteristics of this new outlook of modernity. These are: (1) that the external world of nature does not have to be accepted as it is, but is instead malleable and to a great extent subject to human will and intention; (2) that there is such a thing as an independent self that can decide on its own what it wants—a self that can, by opposing the restrictive world of traditional embeddedness, achieve autonomy and self-sufficiency; (3) that one's place or status in life does not have to depend on ascription, that it is possible to move up or down the social scale according to how well one develops and internalizes a number of qualities not usually emphasized in traditional societies (e.g., systematic planning, single-mindedness, rigorous emotional constraint, etc.); (4) that one's primary orientation should be toward the future rather than toward the past; (5) that the so-called modern era represents a new historical epoch unlike any that has existed before, and though traces from earlier ages may persist, they are now largely irrelevant, since they stem from periods that have been superceded; and (6) that the contemporary age has no choice but to look to itself for its own values, and to "draw its [own] normativity from out of itself."[1] All the inherited guidelines must be either rejected or rethought. The modern individual must learn how to ground him or herself anew, without reference to the criteria of the past.[2]

Attitudes such as these—though espoused by only a few in, say,

1650—received wide assent in Europe and America by 1850. Writing in 1836, for example, Ralph Waldo Emerson probably spoke for the majority of his countrymen when he suggested that there was no longer any need to "grope among the dry bones of the past" now that there existed "new lands, new men, new thoughts."[3] Similar notions were echoed by a whole chorus of American voices in the early nineteenth century, all of them expressing exhilaration at being freed from the burden of tradition, and even from the weight of history itself. The primary emphasis began to be on America as a new country and a new Republic purged of the thoughts, symbols, values and established usages of the Old World. This cleansing, it was assumed, would spark a new burst of creativity as Americans became more original and more independent as a result of being liberated from the dead hand of the past.[4] Back in Europe, the satisfaction of breaking decisively with the past was equally strong. Even more than the Enlightenment philosophes, many in the nineteenth century saw the past as composed of a succession of ages, each of which was entirely *unlike* the contemporary one. Every historical period was said to have its own peculiar configurations, and the social habits and customs that prevailed at any given time in the past were thought to be appropriate only for that time and no other. This being so, there was no need to hold onto the values and traditions of former epochs once those epochs had disappeared into history. Thus, the past came to be regarded as a foreign country and, as compared to the present, a backward one at that. As Bentham put it in 1824, the past by modern standards was full of "abuses and imperfections;" it was a time "much inferior" to the present, and therefore it would be wrong "to idolize, under the name of the wisdom of our ancestors, the wisdom of untaught, inexperienced generations."[5] In Bentham's opinion—and in this he spoke for many—it was preferable by far to embrace the present exclusively in order to forge new values and prescriptions more in line with modern conditions.

As novel as these attitudes might have seemed in the early nineteenth century, there was no sudden lurch from an essentially traditionalist to a modern world view. The transition took place over several generations, and was not even complete by the end of the nineteenth century. Of course, during this span of time many people continued to look to the past, but now they tended to do so for chiefly "modern" reasons: they were inclined (as most still are today) to start with their own experience and then seek out only those precedents from the past that seemed useful; they did not, as was the rule earlier, start with traditional models as the source of truth and then try to make contemporary experience conform to them. When the past is used as a kind of warehouse of potentially useful insights, it may seem that tradition is being honored. In fact it is not, for the sense of real continuity with the past, which needs to be present for a tradition to be authentic, is neither respected nor preserved when the past is approached in such a manner. To return, then, to the two dates mentioned above, one might say that in 1650 the overall cultural framework of the West was traditional. Though emerging areas of modernity existed, they were mostly perceived through traditional lenses. By contrast, in 1850 the overall cultural framework had become modern. Though substantial pockets of tradition survived, they tended to be viewed through the lenses of modernity. Tradition as such had not completely lost its legitimacy, but it was increasingly reconceptualized from a modern perspective. As a result, it was stripped of its "quasi natural status," and hence also of its power to bind social life into an organic whole.

The New Integration: 1880–1920

What had come into existence in the West by the mid-nineteenth century was an essentially *bourgeois world.* All the characteristics of modernity just described helped engender that world, for without modern views of nature, self, discipline, achievement, and the like, the bonds of traditional society would not have been broken, and the lineaments of a new middle-class society would not have come into being.

As the bourgeois world advanced into the late nineteenth and early twentieth century, still other changes occurred. The expansionist processes of state and economy, which previously had followed more or less separate lines of development (especially under laissez-faire conditions earlier in the century), were now increasingly coordinated and consolidated. What had once appeared to be two autonomous tendencies—one political and centered in the state, the other economic and centered in market relations—now not only accelerated but converged. Capital more and more leaned on the state to help open up and protect new areas of investment and to reduce economic imbalances created by the market system, while the state leaned on capital for loans and credit to finance its various undertakings. The logical result of this convergence was that processes which had already taken hold in each sphere (namely, the state's efforts to lift itself above parochial interests, and capitalism's drive to become a world system) now came together in such a way as to advance both of these ends all the more effectively. Not surprisingly, this concurrence of political and economic interests only speeded up the disintegration of many of those traditions which, in spite of everything, had managed to survive into the nineteenth century.

One example of the acceleration of antitraditional processes was the quickening pace of urbanization. In the large cities, everyday existence was radically transformed: the tempo of life became more rapid, contacts with others more fleeting, relationships more transitory. Situations repeatedly occurred which could not be illuminated by previous experience.[6] At the same time, the forces of industrialization also speeded up after the 1880s, thereby engendering what has been called the Second Industrial Revolution. This "second wind" not only meant much greater levels of production, leading to industrial outputs in Europe five to ten times greater than they had been at the beginning of the century. It also meant breakthroughs in technology, electrification, communications, transportation, and applied techniques of scientific management, all of which had the cumulative effect of altering nearly every aspect of quotidian existence. In light of such profound changes, tradition seemed to have even less bearing on contemporary experience than it did several decades earlier.

While these industrial and technical changes were underway, new forms of consumer capitalism also emerged which did not simply disturb the traditional lifeworld—as happened at the time of the first Industrial Revolution—but actually transformed it. At the beginning of the nineteenth century, for example, a complex market system had inserted itself into the center of daily life, thereby disrupting traditional patterns and assumptions. Yet as dramatic as this development was, the market economy only gradually unsettled the world-as-given; it did not produce, instantly and for all elements of the population, radically new "normative orientations."[7] By the end of the nineteenth century, however, a more aggressive consumer capitalism began colonizing the now fragmented lifeworld, forcing it as never before to conform to market directives. The result was an unprecedented plundering and recontextualization of traditional remnants to such an extent that they became little more than inputs in a new system of profit. Old values and modes of life were exploited, objectified, and reified, usually in ways that drained them of their previous meanings.[8]

Alongside this type of colonization there also appeared, thanks to the new industrial and manufacturing capacities of the West, a glut of mass-produced objects which replaced traditional ones in people's lives and homes. With greater abundance and a higher standard of living, it was natural for individuals to want to discard old things rather than make an effort to repair and preserve them. For perhaps the first time in history, large numbers of people had the option of eliminating what seemed to be out of date. But when objects are judged obsolete and thrown away, the presence of the past in daily life becomes drastically reduced and the value of tradition seriously eroded.[9] Even more, as new, purchasable objects began to drive old ones out of circulation, the symbolic meanings attached to enduring things tended to be discredited. As those material objects which recalled long-standing traditions or collective memories became less and less available, people lost hold of a vital means of associative access to the past, and consequently were not induced to think much about tradition. In this way, modern capitalism did not even have to refute tradition; it had only to substitute new things for old ones in order to eliminate the traces and memories of the past. By 1900, what might be called a culture of forgetting—i.e., one based on erasure and an exaggerated notion of obsolescence—was rapidly supplanting a previously dominant culture of remembering.

Accompanying these economic developments were other, more strictly political ones. By the end of the nineteenth century, what had emerged in the West was the modern bureaucratic state—a state freed from many of the constraints that had plagued absolutism a century or two earlier. Of course, by 1900 the various states of Europe and North America had acquired different political physiognomies. Some, like Russia, had remained autocracies; others like Germany and Italy had become constitutional monarchies; and still others, like England, France, and the United States, had become representative democracies. Yet beneath these external forms there was a common, underlying reality: that all Western states had become consolidated, centralized, dynamic, and interventionist. Moreover, they all conceived of their tasks in primarily administrative terms: to regulate civil society, to formalize social relations in legal codes, and to assert governmental prerogatives in nearly every domain of life, including many spheres left untouched by earlier state systems. One instance of this is the way every industrialized state gained a controlling hand in the institutions of primary and secondary education, which had not been the case in earlier times. Through the medium of the school, states were able to introduce precisely the new ideas and national values in which they had a vested interest. Also, by basing its rule on legality and on the simple logic and presumed good will of its procedures, the state increasingly eliminated the need for tradition as a legitimation. True, historicizing claims were resorted to on ceremonial occasions, but at such times the traditions recalled were invariably either those already supportive of the nation-state, or those invented by the state to serve its own purposes. I will return to this issue later, but for now the point is that although some traditions continued to be used by the state, tradition as such lost most of the political utility it once possessed.

As I have indicated, modern capitalism may have been primarily responsible for the exploitation and commodification of the lifeworld, but it joined in partnership with the modern state when it came to organizing and rationalizing it. The nascent rationality Weber detected in the sixteenth- and seventeenth-century bourgeois was eventually transferred to the powerful institutions of state and economy. When this happened, purposive rationality was no longer confined just to the private sphere or to the world of small-scale business enterprises. Instead, it became a matter of large-scale application to the extent that the rationality of the individual subject was gradually objectified and expanded into *systemic* rationality. Once entrenched at the institutional-bureaucratic level, rationality surged beyond and invaded other areas of life as well. It soon became clear that it was the rationalizing imperative of the state even more than that of the market that was bent on conquering and subduing as much of the lifeworld as possible. The reason for this was that in order to administer successfully, the state required rational, predictable behavior on the part of its citizenry, whereas the market was not averse to preserving areas of irrationality that could subsequently be developed for profit. Generally speaking, the bureaucratic state was and still is indifferent to most personality-centered issues of value or meaning in the lifeworld, unless such issues appear to represent a potential threat to state security. What all modern states came to want was correct comportment and compliance with the law; they did not, and still do not, care how law-abiding behavior is arrived at, just that it *is* arrived at. In the meantime, each state, even the most democratic, proceeded to follow the logic of its own rational, inwardly given directives above and beyond the private world of the individual. The net result was that each continued to increase its power, expand its jurisdiction, and extend its system of rules and regulations to the point where there was hardly any leverage left to challenge the authority or legitimacy of the state itself.

As a consequence of these developments, modern nation-states discovered that they had little use for tradition, except perhaps for a narrow but important range of political traditions directly serviceable to them. Therefore, many of those still-extant traditions which could not be co-opted, were allowed either to fall by the wayside or were pushed into oblivion. Though both approaches made sense to the defenders of *raison d'etat* in the nineteenth century, the net effect was an intensive and extensive gutting of the social infrastructure, which in turn produced a greater degree of cultural impoverishment. By eviscerating long-standing traditions, the state, it turned out, had few values to put in their place. It had, on the one hand, the value of rationalization which it did promote, and on the other hand, the value of nationalism, which it cultivated for its own purposes. Both of these were utilized as substitutes for tradition in the hope that they would hold social and political life together, but neither was able to do the job adequately. Rationality alone could not provide enough glue to bind people into a polity; and nationalism, though it worked well in fusing people together in the short term and particularly in moments of crises, could not be counted on to provide stability over the long term. One of the reasons that the state's substitute values were ultimately so ineffectual is that meaning cannot be generated administratively.[10] It is easy enough for a state to destroy or instrumentalize symbolic meanings and values in the lifeworld, but it is much more difficult for it to fabricate new ones. Usually meanings and values have to develop historically over long periods of time within stable communal settings, but it was these very settings that were undergoing wholesale rationalization, partly as a result of the activity of the state itself. Even nationalism, which has been *the* characteristic state ideology of the nineteenth and twentieth centuries, was by no means a creation of the state *ex nihilo*. It assumed its modern form through the careful reshaping of older residues and loyalties which had already been present for generations in the lifeworlds of the West. Hence, even here the state was not as creative as it seemed. It was highly skilled at reassembling and reinterpreting what it inherited, but not at forging something entirely new.

In the generally empty spaces produced by the enfeeblement of tradition, a certain coordination between the nation-state and modern capitalism once again came into play. As traditional communities were emptied of their meanings by a rationalizing state, the market entered the picture to provide a variety of new meanings which helped reintegrate social life at the quotidian level. As a rule, capitalism was and continues to be much freer than the state to transform old values or work up new ones. By offering people a plethora of commodities and an attractive consumer-oriented style of life, market capitalism was able to mobilize whole populations toward new forms of value attachment. But as it happened (and I will discuss this in more detail later), many of the synthetic meanings capitalism created were actually brilliantly conceived simulacra of some of the very traditions the state and economy were in the process of destroying.

Institutional Rationalization

When, by the nineteenth century, reason was institutionalized in outward structures and people came to live and work within these structures, their conduct became increasingly rational and methodical whether they intended it to be or not. Just by being within, or having to respond to, governmental bureaucracies or industrial working conditions on a daily basis, an individual's life activity unavoidably became more efficient, routinized, and rational. It made little difference whether one was at the top of these political and social structures (the government administrator, the corporate executive) or at the bottom (the civil servant, the factory worker); the effect was virtually the same. For built into the very forms of modern institutions were procedures, requirements, regulations, and reward incentives which by their very nature produced rational modes of acting and thinking.[11] As Michel Foucault and others have shown, similar rationalizing patterns and effects could be found by the late nineteenth century in other institutions such as prisons, schools, armies, and hospitals.[12] In every case there was an overflow of formal rationality into areas of social life that had previously been untouched by it.

Initially these powerful rational structures influenced behavior not so much on the level of ideas as on the level of overt conduct—that is, in the way they routinized and instrumentalized human activity. Many subtle and not so subtle forms of coercion were available to authorities to compel rational behavior from without. The kind of methodical, purposive conduct which, among early capitalists, was entirely self-given, could now be imposed on a whole population from the outside by means

47

of institutional controls. Not surprisingly, as modes of external behavior changed, so did modes of perception. To mention only one example here: in the rationalized work situation, the *longue durée* of tradition was gradually condensed into a new approach to time seemingly more appropriate to an industrial setting. Time began to mean the clock time of the working day; or the quantifiable labor time measured by wages yielded; or the rationalized "time table" of schedules relating work to preset goals; or the segmentation of time into its smallest units for maximum utility (as in the time-motion studies of Frederick W. Taylor, which were quickly extended from the factory to the home and eventually to other areas of everyday life).[13] This rationalization of time, which at first was designed only to bring overt behavior into line, gradually seeped into consciousness. Eventually perceptions began to match experience, leading to a temporal foreshortening of the way things were seen and evaluated. In this manner, time came to be conceptualized simply as measured duration, which stripped from it virtually all traces of memory or tradition.

In addition to these changes in time consciousness, there were numerous other "inner effects" that went along with being in daily contact with highly rationalized structures and institutions. An historical perspective on the increasing rationalization of life helps make this point more clearly. In the seventeenth century, the social and political world was assumed to be for the most part irrational. If one wanted to conduct one's life rationally, as the emergent capitalist did, one had to do it on one's own, through inner-directed will and effort. Likewise, during the Enlightenment the assumption was that exterior structures and institutions such as the church or court were embodiments of ignorance and superstition. Reason existed, it was said, but primarily as a transcendental category which could be used to criticize and condemn faulty ecclesiastical or political structures. Only in the nineteenth century did something novel happen, as previously recalcitrant institutions began to succumb to a totalizing rationality. When this occurred, it was no longer possible to regard the social and political world as unreasonable or irrational, as had been the case earlier. Rather, reason now appeared to have become materialized, embodied, and concretized in so many key institutions in the West that what had once been only a dream—the dream of a wholly rational existence—had now become (albeit in distorted form) a palpable reality.

This new situation created an interesting problem. To many in the nineteenth century, the triumph of reason over unreason began to seem like a Pyrrhic victory, since the damage caused by rationalization appeared to outweigh its benefits. But when opposition movements rose up to address the issue of rationalization, many of them fell under the bewitching spell of what they opposed and they ended up becoming rationalized themselves. The labor movement, for instance, began as a protest against, among other things, the rationalization of the workplace, but by 1900 it had itself become bureaucratized and routinized in union and party structures.[14] A number of right-wing movements in late nineteenth-century Europe, such as Ernst Rudorff's "German Movement for the Protection of the Homeland," had also started out by opposing the destructive aspects of industrial rationalization. Later, as larger organizations trying to reach mass constituencies, they became entangled in the same kind of formal, institutional rationality they had once rejected in society at large.[15]

The irony of such reversals was that history appeared to be repeating itself, for it seemed that people were once again being shaped by outside forces and conditions just as they were when traditional society was intact. Modernity first began to rebel against tradition in order to eliminate the pervasiveness of outside determinations; now the same kind of determinations seemed to be returning, only this time with perhaps even more coercive power than before. The irony of the situation was compounded when one recalled that modernity's chief complaint against the societies of the past was that their stifling conformism hindered the development of an autonomous self. And yet almost as soon as the autonomous self emerged under modern conditions, it was threatened by the very force that once appeared to be emancipatory—namely, the force of triumphant rationality.

Responses

The intellectual responses to rationalism had been varied since the beginning of the modern period. In the eighteenth century, for example, most responses were favorable, since rationalization was identified with progress. By 1900, however, a more complicated point of view emerged as both the positive and negative effects of applied rationality began to come more clearly into focus. It was at this time that social critics like Weber began making distinctions between two kinds of rationality: technical and substantive. Technical rationality was described as a reified, mechanical, merely formal type of rationality that is fundamentally amoral, since it concentrates on the perfection of means without asking about ends. Where it takes hold, it destroys without offering anything positive, and yet this was the kind of rationality, so the argument went, that had become ascendant in the modern state and economy. In contrast, substantive rationality was defined as a humane and self-reflexive form of reason that respects ethical frames and contexts, and works organically within them. Whereas technical rationality was said to instrumentalize what it touched, substantive rationality, being informed by "ultimate values" as well as moral and aesthetic elements, was seen as pointing the way to a fulfillment of the highest human potential.[16] For those who held such views, the call was for more rationalization of life, but *only* so long as this meant substantive rationality. The idea of going back to earlier traditional forms was categorically rejected, since in retrospect the world of the past seemed narrow and debilitating. At the same time, the idea of mindlessly affirming the technical rationality of the present was also rejected out of hand. The only viable option that remained was to work to replace technical rationality with substantive rationality.[17]

Also around the turn of the century another kind of response became evident. It came for the most part from neoromantic intellectuals like Stefan George and his circle, who believed that the triumph of rationality was an overwhelmingly negative event in modern history (with *no* distinctions made between good and bad rationality). For those in this camp, the rationalization of life in all its modes was something far worse than the tradition it was replacing. Here the assumption was that rationalization obliterates value as such. But for many of these individuals, the destruction of value and the profound sense of loss it caused awakened a nostalgia for the old traditions and an urge to restore them. The nostalgic outlook on tradition had its roots in early romanticism a century before, but at that time there were still viable traditions extant and available which could be nourished or resuscitated in opposition to rationalization. By 1900 this no longer appeared to be the case, since tradition seemed to have eroded beyond the point of recovery. One had no recourse, then, but to return to it only imaginatively, poetically. The symbols, images, and ideals of the traditional past could yet be recalled and cherished, as they were for writers and poets like Rilke or Yeats, but for most people the hope of actually recuperating tradition itself was largely abandoned.

Yet another noteworthy reaction to rationalization came from those individuals who defined rationalization as the problem, but responded to it by raising new concerns about the "fate of the self." To many around 1900, the supposedly self-reliant, self-determining bourgeois individual of former times had been thoroughly undermined. Moreover, the new kinds of selves that were emerging were said to be increasingly shaped by and dependent on the overwhelmingly impersonal structures of state and economy. Some responded to this development by seeking to strengthen the old, stable, inner-directed self that appeared to be disintegrating. Freud is one example of someone at the time who tried to fortify the ego of the modern individual. One of his central goals was to buttress the weakening sense of self that came not only from inward pressures of the unconscious, but also from the outward pressures and demands of contemporary life. Particularly in his later writings, Freud expressed concern about a "dwindling of the conscious individual personality" under the impact of modern social forces.[18] It seemed to him that the ego, battered and diminished by twentieth-century civilization, needed to be shored up again in order to better perform its function of balancing the conflicting demands of the id, the superego, and the reality principle. In Freud's view, one effective way to shore up the ego was to restore, as an ideal, the old (bourgeois) notion of a centered, self-regulating, autonomous personality—the very type of personality that, as Freud had noticed, contemporary society was in the process of undercutting.

Others, who were Freud's contemporaries and no less concerned than he with the fate of the self in late modernity (e.g., Oscar Wilde in England, Alfred Jarry in France, or Otto Gross in Germany), advocated not so much a rational as a fluid or "porous" self—one many times more flexible than anything usually associated with the Weberian portrait of bourgeois individualism. The modern self, it was said, was becoming a "manipulable object" which needed to be rescued from the conformism that Nietzsche and others attributed to rationalization and the levelling effect of mass society. To those who shared this point of view, the self came to be seen as the last area left where individuality, uniqueness, and real expressivity could still be found. This accounts for the widespread interest from the 1880s on in the notion of "finding oneself," expressing one's "true nature," discovering one's identity, and so on. It was taken for granted that whatever authentic subjectivity one had was hidden beneath the debris of convention. There was presumed to be something like an outer self (rational, status-oriented, shaped by social roles) which invariably obscured or denied an inner self (always vital, spontaneous, creative). This being so, every individual was said to have a responsibility to liberate his or her true self from imprisonment by the false one. If this were done, one would achieve happiness and psychological well-being by becoming a full "personality"; if it were not, one would end up sick, repressed, anxious, and incomplete. (Ideas such as these appeared not only among Nietzscheans, Bergsonians, and vitalist thinkers in Europe between the 1880s and World War I. They were also evident in America among the newly emerging psychologists and "therapists" who at this time began to claim special expertise in understanding the deepest needs and problems of the modern psyche.)[19]

This stress on "loosening up" in order to find one's true identity unwittingly played into the hands of emerging consumer capitalism, which masterfully absorbed and packaged these concerns. In effect, capitalism made the idea of a personality—or the rich inner life that allegedly goes with it—something purchasable if only one bought the right kinds of commodities (now aggressively trumpeted by the nascent advertising and marketing industry).

By means of a single, skillful maneuver, then, modern capitalism at the end of the nineteenth century managed to do two things simultaneously. First, it eliminated the need for the old type of individual (what Sombart called the *Bourgeoisie alten Stils*), even though it was precisely this "old-style bourgeois," with his characteristically purposive-rational approach to life, that helped get capitalist development underway in the first place.[20] This older type now seemed too narrow and rigid to be consumption-oriented; consequently, as industrial capitalism evolved into consumer capitalism, the ideal of the old-fashioned burgher rapidly declined as a model to imitate. Second, modern capitalism encouraged a new and more experimental notion of a self that would be able to live comfortably with ambiguity and uncertainty. In part, the notion of a more flexible self was promoted because the contours of reality were dramatically changing, and people seemed to need more open-ended personality structures to keep up with the dynamics of capitalism itself. But another reason capitalism encouraged a looser concept of self was that there was profit in it. To the extent that people would be willing to reject the old ideal of deferred gratification and throw themselves into the full enjoyment and experience of life, there would be a need for a huge variety of goods and services which the market was ready and able to supply. By the twentieth century, one of the consequences of equating fulfillment with consumption has been an increasingly privatized and self-absorbed form of individualism which is wholly unlike the utilitarian individualism of early modernity. Now there seems to be more of a withdrawal into a commodity-oriented *intérieur*, either because the external world appears so fleeting and ephemeral (and hence not worth one's emotional investment), or because it has become so excessively rationalized (i.e., given over to what Weber called "the cold, skeletal hands of the rational orders").[21]

Not surprisingly, the state and market have responded differently both to the inward turn of the self and to the notion that the self should be fluid and ever-changing. By and large the state has tolerated these two developments so long as, in the political sphere of life with which it is most concerned, behavior is consistent, predictable, and law-abiding. The market, by contrast, has approved of disciplined, dependable behavior primarily in the workplace or on the assembly line, but not in the realm of consumption. As mentioned earlier, the market far more than the state has always opposed too much consistency, preferring instead to keep open some access to the irrational. From the state's perspective, the stirrings of restlessness or unfulfilled longings in a population can signal something potentially dangerous. From the market's perspective, just the opposite is true, for only by nurturing practically every kind of undifferentiated yearning and desire—and then transmuting them into the urge to consume—can the economy stay on an upward course.[22]

Varieties of Modernism

Several developments came to the fore in the West between 1880 and 1920, and each had the effect of undermining tradition. First, broad social-economic tendencies such as the acceleration of industrialization helped to create a new material reality—one which then reacted back upon and eroded earlier traditional contexts. Second, institutional and political trends such as rationalization and the consolidation of the modern state enfeebled many traditional values and practices. And third, a number of intellectual and cultural movements, operating at the ideological level, turned against the old forms and legacies of the past. In the case of the first two developments, the destruction of tradition was often not a specific goal, but merely an unintended consequence of larger processes underway. In the intellectual assault, however, tradition was

usually assailed directly, not inadvertently. If one looks at movements such as vitalism or *Lebensphilosophie,* or at the widespread attack on convention and habit which had become especially intense by the first decades of the twentieth century, it is clear that tradition as "dead life" was explicitly singled out for attack.[23] Here it would be helpful to discuss briefly at least one of these intellectual assaults on tradition around 1900, that of the movement known as modernism.

Modernism as distinguished from modernity may be said to begin with Baudelaire, who was the first to ask poets and painters to commit themselves entirely to the depiction of *la vie moderne.* But modernism as a broad movement in the arts did not get fully underway until the 1880s and after. When it did, the term came to refer to a whole range of parallel and overlapping developments, all of which regarded themselves as "modern," including Symbolism, Art Nouveau, Cubism, Fauvism, Expressionism, *Jugendstil,* Futurism, Imagism, Vorticism, and Dadaism. If one extends the concept beyond 1920, it would also include Constructivism, Bauhaus, *Neue Sachlichkeit,* and Surrealism.

All of these movements set themselves against tradition, and some did so with almost unbounded hostility. Futurism, for instance, demanded the abolition of every line of continuity with the past, including the dynamiting of libraries, museums, and academies, since such institutions were little more than warehouses of dead memories. Dadaism likewise treated surviving traditions as bankrupt. The world, the dadaists said, was in ruins and nothing applied anymore; thus everything handed down through tradition had to be relinquished without nostalgia, including all earlier notions of value, meaning, and memory.[24]

Even among those movements within modernism that were not willing to go this far, there was general agreement on a number of things. For one, it was taken as given that the present age was discontinuous with the past, and that the daily experience of modern life was based on a profound disjunction with what had gone before. It was also assumed that since the present was floating free from the past, everything had become, as Baudelaire expressed it, "transitory, fugitive, and contingent."[25] This being so, one had no choice but to accept and live within the passing moment, not try to attach oneself to anything antedating the present. Finally, all the old artistic and literary forms based upon notions of continuity, organic unity, and historical connection were now regarded as obsolete, since the issues once addressed by tradition were no longer the issues with which the present age needed to be concerned.

In light of these assumptions, the main aspects of the modernist project can now be seen more clearly. They were, first of all, to stress innovation and experimentation in order to, in Pound's words, "make it new!" Indeed, the new-for-its-own-sake became a central category of value for modernism. It is true that earlier artistic movements also spoke of newness and novelty, but when they used such terms they usually meant a simple updating or renovation of traditional genres (as, for example, in neoclassicism or the numerous "renaissances" that have taken place in the West since the ninth century).[26] Previously, then, "new" meant stylistic novelty, or building onto something old and already in place. With modernism the term came to mean *not* the reworking or updating of tradition but "the negation of tradition as such."[27]

Second, with such a great emphasis placed on newness, the idea that one had to "be original" became an issue of critical importance for the writer or artist. Earlier, under the reign of tradition, originality meant establishing or maintaining contact with some origin of inspiration; the closer one got to this primal spiritual source, no matter how it happened to be defined, the more original one was. By the end of the nineteenth century, however, creativity began to be regarded in just the opposite terms: as the act of severing all dependency on the past, distancing oneself from origins, and striking out in directions never explored before.[28] Originality or creativity, it was now said, came through a spontaneous interaction with immediacy. The interaction could take many forms, from sensuous to ironic engagement, but it had to be an interaction with the actuality of present-day experience. To be sure, this did not mean the actuality of life as the man-on-the street understood it, since most modernists treated normal, everyday existence as something banal or vulgar. The merely quotidian contained, after all, the residues and sedimentation of tradition, and was therefore not regarded as anything inspirational. In this respect, virtually all modernists, regardless of political orientation to the Left or Right, were elitist. They wanted to address the immediate problems and issues of the present aesthetically, without reference to prevailing forms of mass culture, which seemed to them stifling in their conventionality.

Last, and given all this, the modernists naturally placed very little value on the concept of repetition, even though repetition as a value had always been integral to the functioning of tradition. In most modernist circles around 1900, the notion that one would want to repeat something already done, even with variations, was generally taken to indicate either a lack of imagination or a lack of creativity. By this time, repetition had come to mean being merely derivative, or holding on to an antiquated past because one had no new ideas of one's own. Since recycling previous models had become anathema, modernism was internally driven to produce a welter of both new forms and new contents. It produced new forms by, among other things, utilizing the materials and the machine images made possible by modern technology; and it produced new contents either by thematizing the concerns of the present over the past, or by making the work of art itself the principal subject matter of art. One result of these developments was to undermine many once-formidable artistic traditions, such as the genre of historical painting which was almost entirely abandoned by modernism. Yet modernism also introduced a wealth of new literary and artistic styles, from the self-reflexive novel to nonrepresentational painting, and each of these innovations has left a decisive mark on twentieth-century culture.

Despite its obvious achievements in the intellectual realm, modernism unintentionally helped open people up to the inducements of a capitalist consumer culture. Beginning particularly in the 1920s, the styles and contents of modernism were absorbed into capitalism, thanks mainly to cultural entrepreneurs who learned how to make use of modernist techniques and symbols for their own purposes. A burgeoning marketing and advertising industry soon drew on the montages, the nonrepresentational forms, and the shock effects of modernism in order to sell commodities to a mass audience. In this way, an aesthetic modernism—which had initially defined itself against both industrial modernity and the market values that supported modernity—was eventually swallowed up by the very forces it once opposed. Of course, it would be wrong to say categorically that modernism was simply an innocent victim of this cooptation, since from the beginning there were components within modernism that lent themselves to the manipulation of the marketplace. One of these was certainly the way that much of modernism wanted, like capitalism, to liquidate "memory, time, and recollection" in order to embrace the new without conflict or restraint.[29] Another was the way the movement wanted aesthetic modes of evaluation and judgment to supercede moral ones. By making value simply a matter of taste, modernism helped weaken the traditional ethical norms which had once served to shore up resistance to precisely the relativism that modern capitalism needed for its success. Both of these modernist components helped detach people from traditional moorings. Hence under the circumstances, it was not all that difficult for the market to utilize modernist impulses, and to do so in such a way as to turn them toward commodification rather than, as most modernists would have wanted, toward purer spiritual or artistic ends.[30]

A Culture of Images

All of the antitraditional tendencies I have been describing in this chapter had come clearly into view by the 1920s. During the next three decades, from roughly 1920 to 1950, these same tendencies were strengthened and consolidated, particularly those associated with political and economic rationalization. After mid-century, however, a number of new developments helped produce a mood still more inhospitable to tradition.

Four of these developments are especially noteworthy. First, the national economies of the West gave way to increasingly globalized modes of production and exchange, which made it less necessary to take account of traditional contexts or incentives. Second, there were major breakthroughs in electronics, microtechnology, cybernetics, automation, and computerization which, taken altogether, moved the West beyond its industrial base into what has been called a postindustrial society. Third, the role of advertising became so pervasive in modern life that it became not merely supplemental to capitalism but integral to it; whereas earlier advertising was important for stimulating and channeling consumer tastes, from the 1950s on it more directly and powerfully molded people's most intimate needs and desires. And fourth, there were revolutionary innovations in media and telecommunications that transformed how information was produced, processed, and disseminated, and how it was received and interpreted. What became especially notable was that events in one part of the world could be transferred instantaneously to almost any other part. Compared to previous ages, modern space and time relations became highly compressed, though the gain in a sense of immediacy or simultaneity was purchased with a loss of a feeling for duration or linear development. In this regard, in the decades since 1950, a visual culture based on electronic images began displacing both the oral and print cultures that preceded it. One result of this development was the rise of television as perhaps the West's major unitary cultural medium—or at any rate, the medium most relied on to provide a common stock of references and a fund of shared values. More than anything else, what now brings together virtually every American regardless of class or background is a familiarity with a whole ensemble of television personalities, as well as with television advertisements, allusions, protocols, metaphors, and modes of expression. The same is true throughout the industrialized West where, by the 1980s, 98 percent of all homes had one or more television sets. It is just because television has become such a natural part of people's lives that it, or rather the fund of information it dispenses, now seems to provide the closest thing we have to a shared *Lebenswelt*. And yet television, even when it unites, does so only fleetingly and synchronically, since it is not particularly interested in nor technically very capable of conveying temporal sequences or continuities. Unlike older cultural formats, its main focus from the beginning has been on the contemporaneous over the traditional, and on the instant impression over the long-term development.

With the ascendancy of a visual culture has naturally come the ascendancy of the image as a primary mode of communication. Again, television has played an especially central role here, as has the whole electronics revolution of the past four decades. Today it is the visual media, including advertising, that help define everything from the roles we play (i.e., what it *looks like* to be a mother or father, a friend or lover) to the popular rituals we conduct (i.e., what it is that should be celebrated or mourned). But what is often not noticed is that the image is not anchored in traditional or historical experience the way the spoken or written word is. Words are steeped in the past; they carry resonances that persist, and they have specific meanings which can be exactly defined. Images, on the other hand, are more easily lifted out of their original contexts and made to mean practically anything one wants. Unlike words, images are volatile and unstable; they carry no precise content or message which can be readily agreed upon, but are instead open-ended and continuously reinscribable with new meanings to replace old ones. The inherent emptiness of images is of course one reason why they are so valuable for certain kinds of communication. Since they have no specific meanings of their own, a variety of meanings can either be projected into or associatively identified with them. Either way, because images are so useful politically and economically the business of producing and circulating them has by now moved into the center of contemporary life. To some critics, the reliance on images seems to have become so extensive today that images appear to have literally merged with "reality" and become indistinguishable from it. Especially for those who spend a great deal of time in front of a television screen, the real may become imagistic and the imagistic real. If this is indeed what has or is happening, then the traces of tradition will surely increasingly disappear from view, since they are neither conveyed nor preserved very well by means of images.

The Postmodern Era

I have been talking about the last three or four decades as an age dominated by the reign of images. Another way to characterize roughly the same time span is to describe it more broadly as a postmodernist period. The term "postmodernism" gained currency in the 1960s with reference to certain tendencies in art and literature, but by the 1980s its meaning was expanded to describe a much more pervasive social and cultural mood within the whole of Western life. Like the modernist sensibility that preceded it, postmodernism celebrates the immediate over the temporally distant, the new over the old, the present over the past. In these respects, at least, it represents an extension—not an overcoming—of modernist modes of thinking. But in other respects, the postmodern outlook seems to move beyond modernism, and to produce something novel. For instance, whereas modernism regarded tradition as a still-powerful force that had to be defeated, this is no longer the case in postmodernism. Tradition is now treated more as a curiosity, as some-thing quaint or interesting. The once-passionate opposition to it has lapsed, because tradition no longer seems to be an obstacle to the emer-gence of the new. Today the sense is that the battle against tradition is over, that modernism was victorious, that the new not only won out but became institutionalized everywhere. This being so, one is now free to be indifferent toward tradition, to discard it as irrelevant, or, if one wants, to casually borrow bits and pieces from it, though without invest-ing them with any special significance.

Similarly, in postmodernism the world of images has been embraced more enthusiastically than before, and yet images are not perceived to be—as they often were in modernism—ciphers to some higher spiritual truth. Rather, postmodernism lays no claim to such things as "higher spiritual truths," so images need refer to nothing in particular, except perhaps to themselves or to other images. In the same vein, postmodern-ism has adopted some notions that were at best only hinted at in modern-ism. One such notion is that the commercialization of art and life is acceptable if it yields aesthetic satisfaction. Another is that for the sake of diversity, it is permissible to mix or recombine the cultural codes by freely blending elements of elite and popular culture. Within postmodernism, distinctions between high and low culture have largely been abandoned. The modernist stress on the sacredness of art has likewise been discarded, making it easier to fuse the "holy" (elite artistic forms and values) with the "profane" (popular forms such as comic strips, advertisements, rock music, and the like).[31] The same kind of transmutation has also occurred with respect to the modernist concept of individualism. The modernists, as I have said, saw the individual as a fluid self, but some elements of postmodernism have gone further and liquidated the very concept of self. The sense now among many theorists of postmodernism is that what we are accustomed to designate as an "individual" is in fact only a multiplicity of forces, desires, and "bodily flows" which have disguised themselves as a unity. Behind this disguise, postmodernists profess to see nothing substantial: neither a centered ego nor a subject with a personal history, but only a chaotic mass of energies and intensities.[32] It is not accidental, then, that so many of these postmodern views of the self, particularly those highlighting the self as a "desiring machine," so closely mirror concepts of the self encouraged by advertising and the prevailing commodity culture. In contemporary capitalism, after all, the ideal consumer is the "subjectless subject" of which Adorno spoke: a self that is "scattered, disconnected, interchangeable, and ephemeral," and hence always ready to become something *other than* what it already is.[33]

When one surveys the postmodern condition as a whole, it becomes evident that postmodernism has moved even further than modernism from the influence of tradition. It is true that there are aspects of postmodernism that *do* return to tradition. Postmodern art and architecture, for example, often quote from the past, and postmodern literature and music borrow from earlier forms. But this kind of return is without real connection, since the goal is not to link up with the continuities of the past, but rather to pull out dissociated fragments from what used to be traditional contexts and then playfully cite or recombine them in new contexts. This has the effect of stripping meaning from the original elements, and then infusing into them new, postmodern messages. The singularities of the tradition may be kept, but only at the cost of completely emptying them of the power they once possessed.

On the whole, then, postmodernism—which may justly be called the "cultural dominant" of the late twentieth century[34]—undermines the spirit of tradition even when it appropriates traditional material. Having little interest in the past for its own sake, and even less in accentuating diachronic tensions between the past and the present, postmodernism tends to dehistoricize most of what it touches. The result of this temporal leveling has been that practically everything has come to subsist on roughly the same plane of value, and to carry roughly the same weight and significance. For those who have some stake in defending tradition, the consequences of these developments have been devastating. As some of these defenders have pointed out, when no distinctions are made between the old and the new—and when in fact the old has been subsumed into the new—then one can begin legitimately to speak about the death of a sense of tradition, if not the death of tradition *as such.*

4 Survivals and Fabrications

The Debris of the Past

The death of tradition. The elimination of tradition from contemporary life. A world now essentially traditionless. These are conclusions reached—perhaps too easily—after surveying the fate of tradition in the West since the seventeenth century.

Present-day commentators who have accepted the story of the demise of tradition are divided into two opposing camps: one celebrates traditionlessness, the other laments it. Both sides offer credible arguments. The first camp affirms traditionlessness because it believes that an age of new realities demands new modes of thought. To rely on tradition as a way of orienting oneself in the world is said to be regressive and harmful, since tradition constricts experience and forces people into old frameworks which become straitjackets. Without tradition, however, a freer and more expansive "protean self" can emerge, a self more in tune with the rhythms of modern life. Traditionlessness is also celebrated because its proponents claim that tradition is little more than a collection of unwarranted biases and bigotries which were the source of inestimable pain and suffering, especially for those who were the victims of powerful religious, ethnic, or patriarchal traditions.

The other camp expresses the opposite point of view. Without tradition, it is said, people are denied a meaningful context in which to function. They lose the sense of continuity and place that only comes with attachments to long-standing collective memories and meanings. Furthermore, without tradition the texture of social life is disrupted, leaving people with nothing but an impoverished feeling of immediacy. Under such conditions, what is called experience lacks foundation and becomes little more than an unintegrated succession of fleeting sensations, none of them linked together through a continuous temporal dimension.[1] Similarly, without tradition a genuine ethical existence is thought to be impossible, since morality cannot be forged anew by every generation based on the exigencies of the moment. For a true moral order to exist there must be a continuous ethical language and a legacy of ethical ideals which, by shaping and interpreting action, actually help produce moral behavior. If such a language and legacy are lost due to the withering away of the traditions that sustain them, there is good reason to worry about the survival of a moral order once the framework of tradition has finally disappeared.

These two positions dominate the discussion of tradition today, but both are based on the erroneous assumption that tradition has been overturned and we are now in a state of traditionlessness. Tradition may have been defeated, but it has not been extinguished. Wherever there is enculturation or socialization there is some element of tradition, and wherever there is a store of background information that people draw upon as tacit knowledge, some amount of tradition is present. What has perhaps been defeated is tradition as social cement, since it is true that tradition no longer holds social life together as it once did. What chiefly binds society now (as we will see in more detail later) are political power, market interests, and media culture. These are the new forces of cohesion that have replaced tradition across a broad front, but this does not mean that tradition itself has been abolished. In spite of everything, some traditions have managed to survive in partial or fragmented form, even within the generally hostile environment of the present. Some endure by retreating from the public to the private realm where they can continue unnoticed in family or neighborhood settings. Others have been withdrawn from the center of society to its periphery and persist unobserved in ethnic or religious subcultures. Still others have been sequestered underground where they maintain a precarious existence beyond the purview of official society. Thus, some traditions have been able to endure because of the will and determination of adherents, who often make great personal sacrifices in order to preserve and remain faithful to seemingly obsolete traditions.

But there is another way traditions survive that has nothing to do with the will or tenacity of individuals. Sometimes traditions survive not by efforts from below but by machinations from above—that is, through the active intervention of the state or market which, for their own reasons, may decide that some traditions ought to be kept alive. If this decision is made, certain traditions that are judged to be useful may be preserved by being rescued from without. These manipulated traditions then continue on openly and publicly, but often at the cost of being distorted and deformed in the process.

Though the terminology may be inexact, I think it is possible to speak of two kinds of surviving traditions: naturally surviving traditions, which are preserved from within the tradition through the fierce loyalty of small groups or collectivities; and artificially sustained traditions, which are preserved from the outside through the operations of political or economic power. In Chapter 8, I will discuss naturally surviving traditions at greater length. In this chapter, however, I will clarify what I mean by artificially sustained traditions, and explain why the state and market choose to preserve some traditions while they simultaneously wage a war of annihilation against others. Before dealing with this specific issue, I want to address—in the following section—a still larger issue, one that should help put the entire matter of surviving traditions into clearer focus.

The Need for Tradition

If one were to ask why traditions come to exist in the first place, the answer so far would be: because they serve some social purpose, because they give order and coherence to collective life. This much is true, but traditions may come into being for another, more subjective reason: because they satisfy some internal, psychological, even visceral "need for tradition."

It may seem odd to speak of a need for tradition, since any claim that such a need exists would appear indefensible. We can prove that there is a need for hunger or self-preservation, but so far no one has proven that there is an inherent need for tradition. Yet as far as we can determine from the historical record, there has always existed in every time and place up until the modern period a multiplicity of traditions. In the light of historical and ethnographic evidence, could it not be said that there must be some powerful underlying need for tradition which has sustained so many traditions for so long? Does not the mere fact that traditions have been continuously present in human experience over millennia indicate that there is and has always been a deep-seated need for them? If such a need did not exist, would they not have been discarded long ago?

Even to attempt to answer these questions adequately would require a different book than this one. Suffice it to say here that, in my view, there is no such thing as a need for tradition *per se,* since nothing in our biological makeup indicates the existence of such a need. However, a number of other basic needs do exist that have been *linked to* or *associated with* a need for tradition, and as people go about satisfying these other needs, they tend to do so through the medium of tradition. For example, a good case can be made that all human beings need to feel secure and protected; they need to be anchored in something dependable and repeatable; they need to feel a part of some meaningful temporal continuum; they need to be connected with their forebears; and they need to have plausible explanations of existence which can dispel fears about the unknown.

Each of these appears to be not a biological, but rather a psychological need, and each seems to have been present throughout history. Taken together they may not add up to a verifiable need for tradition, but because they have always leaned so heavily on tradition in order to be satisfied, it has been natural to regard these needs, however mistakenly, as similar to or synonymous with a need for tradition. For instance, when our ancestors wanted to feel rooted in something secure and dependable, they reached out for tradition. In explaining their behavior, they probably would not have said they wanted security and rootedness, or the other needs mentioned above; what they probably would have said was that they wanted tradition. For if an object satisfies a need (tradition in this case) over a long period of time, eventually it is perceived as the *source* of that need. If this is what has happened historically, it would be incorrect to say that there is some intrinsic need for tradition, even though over the centuries people believed that they experienced such a need. I am suggesting that what they may actually have experienced was a deeper set of needs which they simply translated—or hypostasized— into what *felt to them* like a need for tradition.

Others, like the philosophical anthropologist Arnold Gehlen, have tried to make an even stronger case for the real, as opposed to imaginary, existence of a need for tradition. In a number of works Gehlen has argued that because of the peculiarity of the human condition, mankind has had no choice but to produce traditions in order to survive. According to him, of all the animals, man alone has not developed any specialization of functions that can insure his survival. Unlike all insects and animals, from bees and ants to the higher mammals, man has almost no

65

"true instincts." Constitutionally, he has not been provided with the basic qualities that guarantee self-preservation. Thus, the human species is the only one that is fundamentally unadapted to an environment, the only one that is unfinished, and the only one that possesses what Gehlen calls an essentially "undetermined nature." Rather than follow instincts blindly, man possesses precisely the opposite inclination: he is "world-open," meaning that he is susceptible to a barrage of impressions coming from outside himself. In terms of survival, world-openness is a dangerous attribute, because by being overly receptive to a flood of stimuli from without, the human being remains extremely fragile. In order to compensate, he has to figure out how to maneuvre in a hostile world. Here, paradoxically, his very vulnerability gives him the capacity for development, for by improvising a creative relationship toward his surroundings, man learns how to *appropriate* his world instead of merely operating within it. Through concerted action, he is able to shape and alter his surroundings, thereby creating social and cultural forms which help him survive. Especially important in this respect, man can fashion traditions which then become for him a kind of insulating second nature. In this way, the world, which is otherwise a "field of surprises," becomes a familiar and manageable environment where "impressions and outcomes can be anticipated."[2]

By this interpretation, tradition provides what Gehlen calls "relief" (*Entlastung*). Specifically, the relief provided by tradition screens out or neutralizes an excess of stimuli, thus permitting human beings to function more effectively. In this manner, tradition becomes a supportive substructure, an indispensable ballast for social and cultural life. It sets up a background of habitualized behavior which leads to a certain amount of stability and constancy. Thanks to tradition, man can respond to his world from a template of dependable continuities that he has forged himself—continuities that help him interpret and change the world according to his needs. Tradition, then, becomes an invaluable "directing system" without which human life would hardly be imaginable.[3]

Beyond this view, one can also hypothesize, as Freud did, that there exists an inherent organic need to repeat. Arguably, all human beings harbor an urge to return to an earlier state of existence. Freud called this urge the "repetition compulsion," by which he meant the drive to restore some earlier pleasurable point in time, or even to recapture the original embeddedness at the beginning of life.[4] An individual's departure from this initial embeddedness allegedly produces a reservoir of tension and agitation which in turn activates an impulse to recapture the situation *prior to* the onset of tension. This longing to repeat may not itself be a longing for tradition, but it nevertheless reinforces tradition's importance. For wherever an urge to repeat presents itself, tradition historically has been available to satisfy it.

If the foregoing arguments are at least provisionally accepted, it would seem that: (1) there are certain deep-seated needs in all human beings for security, continuity, and rootedness; and (2) over the centuries these needs have been satisfied by tradition to such a large extent that there appears to exist a bona fide need for tradition. Whether this need for tradition is real or imagined is not the central issue. What matters more is that such a need was *experienced as real* by countless generations of people who were born into and grew up within traditional frameworks. For them there was little doubt that what they felt was a palpable and authentic need for tradition, not some sort of displacement of other needs they could not define. Many of the major institutions of the past, especially cultural and religious ones, made a point of addressing and satisfying this apparent need for tradition. But curiously, neither the early modern state nor the early capitalist market made much of an effort to speak to a need for tradition. So long as tradition was defined as the enemy—as it certainly was from the seventeenth through the nineteenth centuries—the overriding concern was to abolish the need for tradition, not to satisfy it. By the twentieth century, however, with tradition largely defeated and no longer threatening, the state and market have been able to reassess their relation to it. It is not surprising, then, that there has been a new interest in tradition and in the needs it fills. Moreover, since both the modern democratic state and the capitalist market now base their *raisons d'être* on their responsiveness to popular needs and desires, it is imperative that they understand what it is people actually want. If it is determined that people do indeed want tradition, or at least something that feels or looks like tradition, then both would be obligated not only to address this want or need, but to try to satisfy it.

There are essentially two ways in which the state or market can satisfy the need for tradition. One way is simply to keep a number of otherwise precarious traditions alive and intact by propping them up with an extensive commitment of resources, power, and money. However, neither the state nor the market props up just any tradition, but only selected ones, i.e., those that in one way or another can be turned to political or economic advantage. The other way to satisfy the need for tradition is somewhat more complicated. It is based not just on propping up already existing traditions but on actively reworking and reassembling them in such a fashion that they become something other than what they were originally. In this case, a tradition may be extracted from its natural setting, repackaged, and given back to people as authentic. Those who are not familiar with authentic traditions tend to accept such recast traditions as if they were genuine. Even when the need for tradition in a population is wholly legitimate, what is frequently provided by the state or market to satisfy it is only a fabrication.

Both of these processes are ways of artificially sustaining traditions. In the first case, whole traditions are sustained more or less intact with outside help; in the second, it is the reworked parts of an original tradition that are sustained—just enough to give pseudo-traditions the feel of authenticity. To explain how these two processes work, I will first explore the way in which the state addresses the need for tradition, and then the way the market addresses the same need.

The State and Tradition

It may seem strange to consider *any* association between the modern state and tradition. After all, the contemporary bureaucratic state is founded on administrative rationality, and therefore operates primarily on the basis of functional and legal considerations. Concern with tradition would appear to be foreign to its *modus operandi*. Moreover, in the twentieth century the states of the West have increasingly been run by political technocrats and crisis-managers oriented almost exclusively toward the present and future, not the past. The focus today is either on what the state claims it can do for its citizens *now* (i.e., advance the "national interest," raise the level of GNP, lower the unemployment rate, etc.), or on what it promises it can do five or ten years from now by means of its highly touted "steering capacities" and "planning strategies." Because the present and future are so much at the center of attention, one hears little about long continuities that have existed backward in time. Today, paradoxically, every self-respecting state wants to appear both as present-minded and as forward-looking as possible.

Nonetheless, from time to time the normal functioning of the state breaks down. When this occurs, there is usually some recourse to tradition or to the symbols and rhetoric of tradition. At different moments and

68

for different reasons, most modern states experience a "crisis of legitimacy."[5] This can happen when the government fails to assure general economic stability, as was the case in the early and later years of the Weimar Republic. Or it can happen when the state finds itself unable to coordinate major conflicting political interests, as in Russia between 1905 and 1917. If, due to such failures, the state can no longer be sure of the allegiance of its citizenry, it may have to resort to extrapolitical means to secure order and stability.[6] One way to do this is to fall back upon the ballast of tradition. If properly pressed into service, traditions can provide integrative symbols, memories, and associations which are extremely useful in restoring political order. Traditions can also tap a certain amount of emotional-affective support that may prove to be invaluable at critical moments. And perhaps most important, if a state that is in trouble can link itself to powerful political traditions which have allegedly been in existence from time immemorial, it will be able to ground itself in legitimizing concepts having to do with its supposedly fixed existence in time.[7] By identifying with what appears to be historically permanent and unshakable, a state can effectively elevate its stature and buttress its authority in times of strain, or even more seriously, when its very right to exist is called into question.

How does the state harness tradition for its own ends? One way is to put the full weight of its support behind certain surviving traditions— but *only those* that already coincide with the interests of the state. The tradition of nationalism is one such example. It is a fully legitimate, unfabricated, tradition which has existed in the West for several generations. It is also a tradition that, by its very nature, powerfully validates the modern nation-state. Hence it would appear that the state does not have to tamper with nationalism to make it politically effective; it has only to let it alone and nationalism will promote the values the state would want to see developed anyway. Yet, the modern state has not often chosen to take a purely laissez-faire attitude toward nationalism. Rather, it has actively fostered nationalism by institutionalizing it in official ceremonies and public "days of observance," by working it into the legal codes and statutes, and even by ensuring that it is included in school textbooks and curricula. This kind of institutionalization has occurred over the last 100 years or so with regard to traditions of both cultural and political nationalism. States have considered cultural nationalism worth upholding because its emphasis on a nation's shared language, sentiments, ancestral customs and folkways helps stimulate feelings of warmth and *Gemeinschaft,* which are impossible to produce by fiat. Similarly, states have also found it useful to bolster political nationalism because its stress on patriotism, national glory, and the historic greatness of the "fatherland" helps strengthen the state's hand in both domestic and foreign affairs.[8] Both of these nationalist traditions, though they would likely have survived on their own, were actively supported and sustained by the nation-states of the West in the nineteenth and twentieth centuries.

By contrast, when the powers-that-be feel threatened by traditions that seem specifically and obviously *anti*statist, efforts are often made to extirpate such traditions from social and political life, either by legally banning them, or simply by undermining their appeal. One or the other of these responses was evident in the French Third Republic's attack on anarchist and anarcho-syndicalist traditions; in Bismarck's assault on the socialist movement during the Second Empire; and in the war against *narodnik* traditions waged by the Russian state in the late nineteenth century. Likewise, whenever a state notices unfriendly ethnic or separatist traditions within its borders, it is liable to clamp down on them through legal pressure or physical force. Among some of the successor states of the U.S.S.R., as well as in Yugoslavia and many Eastern European countries, one can cite examples of a central government trying to weaken or destroy *staatsfeindlich* traditions, at first by an assortment of repressive measures, but if they fail, by recourse to arms.[9] Finally, if traditions survive that appear to be neutral—i.e., will neither harm nor advance the interests of the state—the state may either try to politicize them or just let them be so long as they remain unthreatening. This last position is the one states have generally taken toward long-standing religious, intellectual, and even political traditions that represent no imminent danger. The state can afford to assume a benign attitude toward such traditions so long as they remain in their own domains and make no universalistic claims that challenge the authority or legitimacy of the state itself.

Another option the state has involves taking remnants from old traditions and refashioning them in such a way as to give them new political meanings. Here the state actually tampers with traditions by extracting symbolically potent residues from the past and identifying itself with them. The state is thus able to harness the meanings or associations these residues evoke, even when this process distorts the original spirit of the tradition. Both the nineteenth and twentieth centuries offer many examples of states adeptly utilizing the vestiges and symbols of tradition in order to arouse powerful feelings, sentiments, and loyalties which could then be transferred to the state itself. In nineteenth-century Switzerland, for instance, traditional religious hymns were nationalized by replacing the original lyrics with patriotic ones. Hence, words like "Nation, Nation, wie voll klingt der Ton" were inserted into previously religious songs, and then taught in school as national hymns. The stirring emotional charge still resonating from the song's earlier life helped deepen the patriotic feelings evoked by the song in its newer form.[10] Likewise, in France numerous ceremonies, *fêtes,* and holy days, all rich in traditional communal meanings, were deftly appropriated by the state and then invested with national political meanings.[11] When transformations of this kind are done successfully, the fragments of old traditions are lifted from their previous settings, drafted for new purposes, and re-presented to people as if they were authentic national traditions of long duration. Not the least result of this process is that people lose sight of the actual nature of an expropriated tradition and learn to develop commitments not to the traditions as they once were, but to their reconstructed facsimiles.

Finally, the state has yet another option. Beyond absorbing surviving traditions or tapping the symbolic power of defunct ones, it can invent traditions when the need arises. A tradition is invented when the state fabricates continuities regarding the state's triumphal march through history in order to increase national consciousness and strengthen the bond between the state and its citizenry. An invented tradition is created out of false memories of the past which are imposed on the lifeworld from the top down. If people come to accept such memories as true, the state naturally gains the appearance of greater historical depth and its prestige is enhanced accordingly. Since at least the time of the French Revolution, virtually all modern states have invented traditions in order to provide themselves with a usable past. In England, for example, the traditional pomp and pageantry now associated with the British monarchy gives the impression of dating back centuries. In fact, most of the rituals surrounding state events like the coronation were forged in the nineteenth century with the express purpose of suggesting lineage back to the Middle Ages.[12] Fake continuities were also manufactured by the French Right in the early twentieth century (e.g., *Action Française's* so-called tradition of "les maitres de la contre-révolution"),[13] and they were produced again on a more massive scale by the Nazi regime in the

71

1930s. Of all the new states of the West in the modern period, the U.S.S.R. stood practically alone in showing little interest in creating artificial traditions to bolster its legitimacy.[14]

Overall, then, most modern states have noticed what appears to be a need for tradition in people, and they have addressed this need by appropriating, reifying, or instrumentalizing useful tradition; where these methods have not worked, they have invented them. In all of this, the state's involvement with whole or partial traditions has not been gratuitous, but calculated. In addressing what is apparently a deeply engrained popular longing for tradition, states have all too often utilized this longing for their own ends and purposes. The result, it seems, has not necessarily been more satisfied people, but only more powerful states.

Capitalism and Tradition

Modern capitalism has also turned tradition to its own advantage, but in ways different than the state. As the dominant mode of production and exchange in the West, capitalism has tended not so much to instrumentalize tradition as to commodify it, to transform it into an object that can be packaged and sold.

As a rule, capitalism seems to be more hostile to tradition than the state is. The reason: capitalism thrives on novelty. It has a vested interest in rapid and continuous change, where the old is repeatedly thrown out and the new installed. The worst thing that can happen is for people to cling to obsolete historical memories, or stay locked within narrow patterns of behavior, since this would discourage the inclination to buy. As Marx correctly pointed out, a market economy is fueled by the need to dissolve all "fast-frozen relations" which only act as a brake upon the drive for profit. If capitalism is to work properly, the way has to be prepared for a constant dislodging of habit, and a continuous expansion of desires and expectations.

With this in mind, it would appear that tradition should be of little use to capitalism. What is more, the modern market—to an even greater extent than the modern state—is interested not in the distant past but in the present or the near future, since it is the demand of the moment that turns a profit. The planning horizons and production schedules developed in corporate boardrooms are naturally not directed backward toward historical continuities, but forward to the months and years ahead.

72

In a word, economic advancement depends more on prognosis than retrospection.

What then is capitalism's relation to tradition? In most respects capitalism seems indifferent to tradition, since its predominant inclination is to exploit the new lifestyle needs which it helps define and then attempts to satisfy. Yet the perceptive capitalist entrepreneur or merchandising expert recognizes that there also exists among people today, no less than in the past, something that resembles a need for tradition. Whenever such a need is detected, a certain kind of market logic goes into operation: a logic which dictates that where a need exists it ought to be addressed, and that to address it is to subsume it under the commodity form. Obviously, if what looks like a longing for tradition could be transmuted into a longing for objects that *suggest* or *represent* tradition, a great deal of money could be made. If, for instance, the yearning for stability or continuity could be converted into the longing for the "good old days," and if the good old days could be identified with certain marketable products, then the need for tradition could be successfully drawn into the sphere of consumption. As William Leiss and others have demonstrated, this kind of commercial sleight-of-hand is accomplished very adroitly. For example, the tradition of neighborliness in small-town life is portrayed in background settings in television commercials. The people in such commercials are shown participating in different forms of interaction within traditional and still intact *Lebenswelten* which are made to look highly appealing. The product to be promoted is then set *in* this lifeworld context in such a fashion as to receive, through proximity, some of the emotional power of the traditions that surround it. This, it is assumed, makes the product more attractive and desirable. In buying the product, a consumer may be buying not the commodity itself but its inferences to the traditions of small-town life—even though, in reality, those very traditions may have long since disappeared.[15]

Nothing in this century has promoted "modern values" more aggressively than capitalism, but the managers of the economy have lately sensed an uneasy acceptance of these values. This uneasiness stems from the discomfort many people now feel in the midst of the complexity and impersonality, the speed and nervousness, of daily existence. It is only natural to attribute these negative feelings to a profound estrangement from the less anxiety-ridden world of tradition. In response to this sense of dissociation from the past, or more exactly, from the warmth and security the past represents, advertisers and marketing strategists have ransacked the storeroom of tradition for material that can soothe modern disquietude over the absence of connectedness or community.[16] This material, they have found, can be condensed into images, and the images then linked associatively to salable objects (in the way I have described with respect to small-town life). When what were once real traditional practices or values are turned into images, something that was actual or palpable becomes merely illusory. Thus, formerly vital traditions are converted into iconic images that are not themselves traditions but simply refer to them. As people consume the images of tradition, they may come to think that they are acquiring the traditions themselves, but they would be mistaken, for images are always and only representations. At best, images can only allude to traditions, but when they do, they tend to capture a tradition's most superficial aspects, for example its form or mood but not its substance. At some level of awareness many people realize that representations are not adequate substitutes for traditions, that they are unable to satisfy the deepest human cravings for security or rootedness. Because of this inherent inadequacy of images, some individuals have tried to recapture "real" traditions. But this attempt at recovery is more difficult than one might suppose, for to the extent that images of tradition are presently replacing actual traditions, a massive deflection is taking place, making it hard for people even to detect, let alone retrieve, authentic traditions.

Nonetheless, the importance of images for modern capitalism cannot be emphasized strongly enough. More than words, images penetrate the unconscious where they are able to affect behavior at the deepest levels of the personality. By comparison, although verbal messages may contain more exact information, they usually register no deeper than the conscious layer of the ego.[17] For this reason, images are useful in arousing a plethora of desires which can subsequently be satisfied through consumption. So central have the production and distribution of images become for the ongoing success of contemporary capitalism that they, along with the industries they have spawned, are now part of the substructure, and not merely the superstructure, of modern life.

To the extent that there has been a breakdown of the old symbolic order of the West, new images have been called upon to provide some degree of social cohesion. Consumer advertising, in particular, has responded by creating a symbolic system of reference and coding so extensive that it appears to have subtly worked its way into the modes of thought and perception of everyone who has daily contact with the mass media. Though it is true that most of the images circulated are about the present and present-day hopes, expectations, and desires, many are also about the past, and their function is to tell us how we should think about what has gone before. Today, perhaps more than ever, it is through images that we learn who we are and convey to others who we are. We learn to identify the character of other people by the images they consume, and to assess their relationship to us by how they relate to images. Hence, the acquisition and display of images has become an essential ingredient of social communication and social integration. Where tradition once provided a dependable source of cultural connection, today it is advertising and electronic images that are called upon to perform the same role.

Just as modern capitalism has discovered how to compress traditions into images and attach images to commodities, it has also discovered how to do the same with regard to the past in general. Yearning for the past, or for a particular moment in the past, is what people now call "nostalgia." Nostalgia, of course, was not invented by capitalism; as a particular kind of sentiment, it has existed since archaic times. But it was not until the contemporary period that nostalgia was appropriated by market forces and turned into a source of profit.

Wherever "modern" nostalgia exists,[18] it always contains two essential components: first, an intense desire to return to some time or setting in the past that was more fulfilling; and second, a tendency to idealize that earlier moment by selectively crystallizing its elements in such a way as to make it more attractive than it actually was.[19] Both of these components lend themselves to commodification. In our own time there has even emerged a nostalgia industry, fed by advertising and the media, which thrives even in this supposedly traditionless age. The nostalgia industry operates by seizing upon natural impulses to recall and cherish the past. But it attempts to satisfy these impulses not so much with accurately restored material as with easily apprehended clichés and formulas that merely represent but do not authentically reproduce the past (e.g., the Old South, the "gay nineties," the "roaring twenties").

Sometimes the past as it really was is mined for useful scraps of sentiment which are then reassembled and prepared for sale. In this case, at least, some legitimate elements of the past are brought forward, no matter how badly distorted. But sometimes the commodification of nostalgia can take on an even more questionable form. An image of what advertisers or marketing experts think the past must have been like can be created *in* the present, *for* present consumption. The image may have little or nothing to do with the past itself, but may simply be concocted in the present and imputed to the past, perhaps because it is thought that people want or need to think about the past in a particular way. When this happens, it is not the past or its traditions that are reified, but only an imagined version of what the past *should* look like if it is to conform to contemporary expectations.[20] (This is how stylized images of "rural wholesomeness" are manufactured in order to sell whole-grain cereals, or how glossy images of Western "rugged individualism" are produced to sell cigarettes.)

In this respect, the market's creation of a pseudopast or of pseudo-traditions is the economic equivalent of the state's invention of tradition. In both, no messages are really received from the past. Rather, present-day messages are inserted into the past and then supposedly recovered; but what is actually recovered is only the present's conception of the past. That so many people today seem to accept the fabricated images of the past as authentic, and consequently experience the past mainly in synthetic form, may be some indication of how far the present age has lost touch with the actual past and its traditions.

I began this chapter with the concept of the "death of tradition," but then suggested that we are not as traditionless as it might at first seem. Despite the fact that many traditions have been turned into images, a number of whole or partial traditions have persisted into our own time. So far I have mentioned three ways in which such traditions have survived (and in a later chapter I will mention a fourth): by being artificially propped up with outside help, by being instrumentalized by the state, and by being commodified by the market. It is important now to shift the discussion away from how or why traditions have persisted and focus on the predicament of enduring traditions in the modern age. In the next chapter, I specifically address the problem of how to respond to living (and dead) traditions by suggesting how we might reassess their value and importance within the context of modernity.

5   Rethinking Tradition

Rescue Operations

All traditions today exist in one of the following three conditions. First, there are traditions that have been destroyed or dismantled as active processes, but which continue on as fragments of value or behavior outside their original contexts. Second, there are traditions that persist at the center of social life, but at the price of being rationalized by the state or commercialized by the market. Last, there are traditions that endure more or less intact, but primarily at the margins of society, and within a greatly diminished sphere of influence.

Of the three conditions in which traditions currently find themselves, it is the first that I will focus on here. (I will return to the other two conditions at the end of the chapter.) My concern is with those social, cultural, intellectual, political, and religious traditions that have lapsed or been eliminated as ongoing processes, but which are still knowable through their surviving remnants. What attitude should one take toward traditions such as these, which have either faded away or been expunged, but which have nevertheless left some traces behind?

At present, probably the most familiar attitude toward surpassed traditions is a flatly dismissive one which assumes that what has perished ought simply to be buried and forgotten. Another attitude, warmly embraced by romantic conservatives, is exactly the opposite. It asserts that the traditions of the past offer better guidelines for life than what we have now, and consequently it sentimentalizes the old traditions and longs to return to them. Still another attitude toward bygone traditions is one that remains firmly grounded in the present but finds value in bringing traditions into a modern setting. Here the past is sought out not to escape into it, but to perform what might be called a "rescue operation."

In my view, this last relation to tradition is the most compelling, because it neither discounts former traditions as irrelevant, nor flees to them for emotional support. Instead, it tries to salvage certain outmoded traditions by asking what they can contribute to solving contemporary problems. This reclamation of discarded tradition is what I mean by a rescue operation. Of course, there are right and wrong ways to salvage the past; not every rescue deserves approbation just because it involves an effort at recovery. After all, both the state and the market remain fixed in the present, and yet try to rescue the past, but as I have pointed out, they do so in manipulative and exploitative ways. Among other questionable attempts at salvaging the traditions of the past has been an aesthetic mode of rescue, whereby traditions are "saved," but only in order to transform them into beautiful *objets trouvé* to be contemplated from a distance. Another is the ironic mode of rescue which retrieves traditions in order to playfully rearrange their meanings in new combinations.[1]

In addition to these approaches to past traditions, both of which have gained currency mainly among literary and artistic elites, there are two other dubious types of rescue, both of which have found their greatest appeal outside the sphere of the avant garde. One is to salvage the past by means of "traditionalism," and the other is to recuperate tradition through the study of history. By noting what is lacking in these last two types of rescue, it will be easier to identify the right way to contact discontinued traditions.

Traditionalism

As an ideology, traditionalism opposes the present in its entirety and looks to past traditions for an alternate way of being. This backward glance, however, is not wistful or escapist, but militant and activist, for traditionalism's primary goal is to bring about a coercive restoration of "the way things were." In its purest form it attempts literally to set the clock back in order to make the past come alive again in the present. Traditionalism's underlying assumption is that the world governed by tradition was simpler, better, and morally healthier than the world we have now. This being so, tradition should not just be fondly recalled, but radically repeated. Yet for tradition to become operative once again, modernity would have to be eradicated so that the normativity of past traditions can be restored.[2]

Traditionalism usually crops up in situations where a modern, tech-

78

nical-industrial culture has been superimposed on an older, traditional one. In the nineteenth and twentieth centuries, traditionalist movements have most often emerged in colonial settings as a response to Western imperialism. But some have also appeared within the West itself, particularly among disgruntled elements of the peasantry or aristocracy. Within such classes or strata of the population, traditionalism provides at least one answer to the problem of cultural and economic dislocation. This answer demands not just a restoration of the spirit of the past, but a dogmatic restoration of the very letter of the traditions as well. In late nineteenth-century Germany, for instance, such traditionalist tendencies were evident in parts of the old Junker class and the German *Bauerntum*. Both the landed gentry and the peasantry produced spokesmen who defended a highly idealized picture of a preindustrial past which seemed to be vanishing under the pressure of capitalist modernity. Based on this idealized picture, it was easy for extremist intellectuals to call for a reinstatement of the traditional values and corporate structure of a bygone era.[3] Nazi ideologues later elaborated on the traditionalist repertoire of ideas and images in such a way as to invent a mythical *Volksgemeinschaft* stocked with organic, integrative traditions. In making a pitch to the peasantry, the Nazi party implied that it would reconstitute a traditionalist lifeworld if and when it came to power. It seems likely that many peasants were drawn to National Socialism because they perceived it to be a traditionalist movement of restoration, which of course it was not.[4]

Generally speaking, there appears to be an uncompromising rigidity built into the outlook of traditionalism precisely because its resentments against the forces of the contemporary world are so intense. Ironically, though traditionalism is based on a rejection of modernity, it can come into being only *within* modernity. Traditionalism makes no sense otherwise. Defining itself exclusively in relation to what it opposes, traditionalism is modernity's negative side, and as such cannot clearly separate itself from what it repudiates. Moreover, if a forced restoration of tradition were to come about, the help of a powerful, centralized state would be essential, since it is unlikely that old values or practices could be recycled without some amount of institutional coercion. But the contemporary bureaucratic state, itself a product of modernity, could not be counted on to serve antimodern ends. Perhaps it might do so for a short while, but over the long duration a statist traditionalism would be a contradiction in terms.

Equally troubling is the fact that traditionalism, despite all its pro-
fessed interest in the past, is fundamentally ahistorical. It assumes that
earlier traditions can simply be reinstated in the present, without taking
into account intervening developments which effectively make that
option impossible. In fact, tradition cannot be reestablished by fiat. It can
only regenerate when the entire network of relations that once engendered and sustained tradition is recreated intact. But such a feat of
temporal reconstruction is beyond imagining. The underlying conditions that once nourished old forms of life have receded into the historical past and are now unrecoverable. They have been superseded by new
conditions whose very nature prevents any compulsory restoration of
the old traditions.

The Study of History

The study of history is a less extreme, but equally inadequate, way of
rescuing vanished traditions, for what it offers is essentially a cognitive
reappropriation of the past. Through historical consciousness one can
become knowledgeable *about* the traditions, but this in no way guaran-
tees that salvaged traditions will be brought to bear on present problems.

It is much easier to draw this conclusion today than it was in the
nineteenth century, when a great deal of hope was placed in history as
the rescuer of tradition. Two distinct modes of rescue were then envi-
sioned. The first was a rescue of the *contents* of tradition. Here the
historian was entrusted with the task not only of re-collecting the mi-
nutest factual details of fading traditions before they disappeared altogether, but of preserving some sense of their feel and texture for future
generations. A type of history known as historicism did this especially
well.[5] It captured and lovingly conveyed what it was like to live inside
previous traditional frameworks—something that, by the nineteenth
century, was becoming increasingly difficult to achieve *in reality*. The
problem, however, was that historicism had no choice but to turn what
was once the actual experience of tradition into mere information. This
was the price that had to be paid to preserve what was disappearing.
Unlike traditionalism, which believed that all traditions were in principle repeatable, historicism accepted the irreversibility of time. What was
slipping away might vanish forever unless the historian could rescue the
past *mentally* by remembering it as photographically as possible.

This concern with exact recollection in order to save tradition from oblivion was centrally important not only to historicists but to their folklorist counterparts as well. The folklorists also sought to preserve what they could by remembering and recording spent traditions in precise detail. It is therefore no accident that so many journals of folklore research were founded in the nineteenth century. One of the chief goals of such journals, as many of their titles indicate (e.g., *La Tradition, Revue des traditions populaires, Revue du traditionisme français et étranger,* etc.), was to keep alive an awareness of the specifics of the traditional past before they were lost sight of completely.

The second mode of rescue was an attempt to salvage not so much the content as the *form* of deteriorating traditions. Here the historian was called upon to grasp and communicate the whole rather than the details, with the whole meaning the epic totality of the past, or what Ranke called "the connectedness of history in the large."[6] With tradition eroding, there appeared to be no cohesive force that could hold together Western culture and society. But the hope was that if the historian could write a kind of history that stressed the overarching continuities, the organic connections, and the temporal sequences that still bound the past to the present, then history could perhaps provide the unity that tradition itself had once supplied. Through its grand narratives of the *longue durée,* history might even become the functional equivalent of tradition. Such at least was the hope, but it was a vain one. The world was indeed becoming fractured, and history was unable to piece it together again, for merely to tell the story of the unfolding of tradition can never be as integrative as tradition itself.

What to replace fading traditions with was one problem that nineteenth-century historians were never able to solve. Though they realized that the traditions, once gone, could never be restored exactly as they were, historians could do little more than offer history as a substitute for them. But history, as it happened, was a rather unsatisfactory substitute. For one thing, it objectified what it purported to rescue by transmuting traditional practices and beliefs into knowledge acquired at a distance. For another, history's "rational gaze" effectively stripped tradition of exactly those irreplaceable qualities that traditionalism had most wanted to protect: its sacredness, its mystique, and its unchallengeable authority. In this respect, history as information *about* tradition seemed to eviscerate the very thing it attempted to preserve.

There was yet another problem with history as a mode of rescue. Not only could it suggest nothing but itself as a weak replacement for tradition, but eventually much of what history described as tradition turned out to be a different series of events than those which had actually constituted the traditions.[7] Not all nineteenth- and twentieth-century history, but a good portion of it, falsely reconstructed the traditions of the past, and thereby fundamentally misrepresented them. By this I mean that the narratives many historians related did not focus on the traditions considered essential by the people who lived within them. Rather, the historians focused on the traditions that seemed most crucial to them as historians—and in deciding what was crucial they were, of course, decisively shaped by their class, social position, and intellectual training. Consequently, the details of the traditions they recounted or the continuities they described were generally only those that the historians believed were worth remembering, and too often these had little or nothing to do with the communal traditions that the people *inside* of them would have wanted to preserve.

For probably the majority of nineteenth-century historians—but not the majority of nineteenth-century people—the important traditions were the political ones leading up to the triumph of the modern nation-state. Of all the traditions to be cognizant of, it was the national traditions that people were primarily enjoined to recall by the most prominent historians of the nineteenth century, including Treitschke and Sybel in Germany, Thiers in France, Seeley in England, and Bancroft in the United States. Thanks also to the rise of state-sponsored public education in all the countries of the West at this time, these patriotic traditions were also the ones that became institutionalized in the primary and secondary schools.[8] As people "learned history," they recalled mainly the political succession of events, but forgot many of the other traditions whose histories were not considered important enough to record.

By the late twentieth century, it is easier to see that the study of history has, at most, given us only knowledge about tradition. It has increased our factual and even our conceptual awareness of the past to such an extent that we now have incomparably more information about the traditions than we have ever had. Furthermore, because of recent achievements in social and cultural history, it is not just the political traditions that we know in such detail but many others as well. And yet, despite all this, we feel far less identity with these traditions than did our ancestors. Though we know objectively what many traditions looked like, how they functioned, why they emerged, and how they disappeared, we experience little sense of continuity or connectedness with them. One of the reasons for this is that to cognitively "know" a tradition, and to really and fully belong to or internalize it, are two entirely different things. In the last analysis the formal study of history encourages only the first.

None of this means that there is something inherently wrong with studying history, or something harmful about historical consciousness. It simply means that history in and of itself is not capable of rescuing tradition in the most meaningful sense of the word. To ask this of history is to invest it with a heavier weight of responsibility than it can reasonably bear.

Tradition and Otherness

If traditionalism and the study of history are unsatisfactory ways of rescuing discontinued traditions, how should a rescue be made? To answer this question, one needs to recall some of the reasons why salvaging eclipsed traditions is important in the first place. It is important because, more than anything else, tradition provides a sense of place, and therefore a certain amount of ontological security. It is important, too, because tradition is the locus of a wealth of nonrenewable, nonrepeatable values which are obtainable only by inheritance. And finally tradition is important because it lends depth and richness to experience. All of these are valid reasons for wanting to rescue the traditions of the past.

But there is yet another reason for getting in touch with such traditions. Unlike those just mentioned, this one has only surfaced along with modernity itself. This new reason suggests that salvaging lapsed traditions is important precisely because such traditions now represent something *other than* what they represented to preceding generations. In earlier times, as I have already indicated, tradition was a natural and familiar part of everyday life. Thus, being in contact with it provided warmth, security, normativity, rootedness, and continuity. But today the very traditions that were once vital and integrative are regarded as merely historical phenomena. To the extent that the passage of time has forced us to view them across a wide temporal gulf, our sense of connectedness with them has snapped. The same traditions our predecessors knew intimately now represent strange or alien forms of life which are strikingly different from those we are acquainted with in the present. But just because our perceptions of the old traditions have changed does not mean that those traditions are no longer significant. Nor can we say that we need them less because, by present-day standards of valuation, they have been judged to be obsolete. On the contrary, it is just because extinguished traditions now embody something "other" instead of something familiar that they have become especially important.

Human beings have always sought contact with otherness. In earlier epochs they did so by trying to fuse with the sacred, or experimenting with altered stated of consciousness, or seeking adventures in unexplored places or unstructured situations. Always the quest was for mystery beyond security—that is, for something so different that an encounter with it would call into question the normal boundaries of daily life. Sometimes, as with mystics and holy men, the quest for difference was directed toward a Transcendental Other defined as God, the numinous, or the *mysterium tremendum*. Sometimes the quest was directed toward the profane otherness of alien peoples and customs (a role, for example, that the Scythians played for the Greeks, the ancient Germans for the Romans, and the New World "savages" for seventeenth- and eighteenth-century European travelers). And sometimes, finally, the quest was directed toward the sexual other, or toward an otherness deeply embedded within the psyche or the unconscious.

All of these are modes by or through which encounters with otherness have occurred, and still occur. But now, due to the deep fissure separating the past from the present, a new source of otherness has emerged in the form of expired or terminated traditions. Paradoxically, by contacting the very same traditions that our ancestors once experienced in a direct and immediate way, one gains not a sense of rootedness but a sense of profound *difference*. The dilemma that follows from this is a serious one, for if former traditions now represent otherness, they cannot provide what they have always provided historically: namely, a sense of continuity, location, sedimentation. Something cannot be radically other and yet at the same time provide security and embeddedness, for by its very nature, what is other disturbs rather than comforts. As those traditions which once gave people a feeling of warmth and security slip into the past, they become manifestations of difference. But contrary to the usual arguments, this does not make them irrelevant. Rather, it makes them all the more essential, for today no less than in the past we still require powerful encounters with alterity, and we now have tradition available, as our predecessors did not, to give us another medium through which to achieve such encounters.

Having said this much, I want to clarify two points about tradition. First, there is no such thing, at least not in our profane world, as otherness per se. What is called "other" is always relative to where one happens to be. What appears to be wholly different is in part determined by the framework of an individual and his culture. Thus, other is simply the opposite of what seems most familiar. The so-called primitive peoples of early ethnographic description were categorized as other because their exotic habits and beliefs seemed so abnormal by Western standards of evaluation. By the same token, lapsed traditions stemming from our own cultural past can appear as other when they represent ways of being with which we are no longer directly acquainted. Nevertheless, a careful observer should be able to distinguish greater or lesser degrees of otherness in various traditions. For example, those traditions that receded a century or so ago may now be viewed as other, but they do not seem as unfamiliar as those traditions that disappeared several centuries ago. The reason for this difference is, of course, that recently discontinued traditions, even when inactive as traditions, still reverberate in the culture. Because references to them continue to be made after they have disappeared, they may seem strange or foreign to us, but not incomprehensible.

By contrast, an encounter with the archaic traditions of the distant past would be much more unsettling, because their very remoteness would make their differences that much more pronounced. If, for instance, one were to make contact with the vanished traditions of ancient Greece—the traditions that were overtaken more than two millennia ago by the classical heritage that triumphed in the West—one would no doubt be shaken by how radically different those traditions were. The scholarship of E. R. Dodds, Jean-Pierre Vernant, Pierre Vidal-Naquet, Marcel Detienne, Walter Burkert, and others has begun to make accessible these defeated traditions, and the more they are known, the clearer it is that there was an alternate Greece to that of Pericles and the Parthenon. The traditions of this prerational Greece were savage, barbaric, and tribal. They expressed a Mediterranean-sexist "culture of masks and death, ritual ecstasies, slavery, scapegoating, [and] phallocratic homosexuality," and hence they were, at their core, "utterly non- or anticlassical [with] something of the electrifying otherness and fascination . . . of the Aztec world."[9] Obviously, an encounter with such ancient traditions would give one a more startling experience of profound difference than would be the case with traditions abandoned only three or four generations ago.

85

The first point I want to make, then, is that perhaps we should distinguish between those traditions that were depleted or destroyed long ago and those that have succumbed relatively recently; though both may embody otherness, some embody it to a more extreme degree. A second point is that the modern culture industry has discovered that most people seem to need some contact with otherness, just as they appear to require contact with tradition. The culture industry has tried to respond to this need for otherness by providing at least small doses of it to the consuming public. But because of its inherent limitations, the culture industry (and the market in general) can never do this successfully; it can only offer reified, but not authentic, forms of otherness. For otherness to be authentic, it must have its own integrity and legitimacy, it must speak with its own voice and on its own terms. But this is exactly what the culture industry does not and cannot allow. The electronic media in particular has become adept at appearing to convey otherness, but always in carefully controlled amounts—that is, just enough to address a yearning for difference, but not enough to put at risk the basic structures of modern life. Thus, the small slices of otherness that are made available in mass cultural formats are either very carefully framed (as with the exposure of tabooed material on TV talk shows, or the "aberrant," but still acceptably deviant, lifestyles of rock stars), or are actually manufactured by the market itself (the extensive pulp literature of violence and sexual deviance). In both cases, otherness is presented primarily as a form of entertainment to counteract the "deadly sameness" of everyday life, but the result is a radical dilution of the true power of difference. What one ends up with today in commercialized culture is not real otherness but "artificial alterity."[10] Whereas an encounter with real otherness has the capacity to make one question one's normal assumptions and assurances, an encounter with the pseudo-otherness of the culture industry only confirms and reinforces the world as it is.

These remarks should explain why I value otherness, especially the otherness represented by tradition. We need to recuperate past traditions not to restore a previous set of norms, as traditionalism tries to do; and not to impose new forms of social integration, which tradition is now incapable of achieving in any case; but to gain access to what might be called the *unheimisch*. I use this term because it clearly expresses what the otherness of tradition seems to offer. The word *unheimisch* literally means that which is "non-home" (*un-heim*), i.e., alien or foreign.[11] As the poet Friedrich Hölderlin pointed out, if one wants to grasp what is at hand, it is essential to experience what is distant or *unheimisch*, even to the extent of temporarily losing oneself in it. Only by coming back from what is different—only, that is, in "homecoming"—is it possible to comprehend what is familiar. For in returning home, the ordinary or everyday is viewed anew in light of what is foreign, and in this way it is perhaps seen clearly for the first time. If those traditions that have receded into the past are regarded as *unheimisch* because they now seem strange or other, the same point holds: we cannot fully know what we experience around us except in relation to what is profoundly different, including the difference of the traditions that have been left behind. Thus, an encounter with temporal otherness would be necessary to transcend a one-dimensional understanding of ourselves and our age. According to Hölderlin, Germans of the early nineteenth century would have to encounter the otherness of the ancient Greeks, for only by passing through and lingering for a while in *that* distant foreign land could a German, particularly a German poet, journey back to his own homeland and finally comprehend it. As Hölderlin saw it, the goal should be neither to discard the otherness of the past nor to return to it in order to be at home there. Rather the goal should be to confront the *Heimische* (the normal, the everyday) with the experience of having known the *Unheimische*, for it may be only in this way that the present can be fully grasped and understood.[12]

Tradition and Critique

The most valuable thing that tradition can offer, then, is "an imaginative entry into an alien turn of mind."[13] Being acquainted with the otherness of spent traditions not only makes possible a better understanding of modernity, but it also lays the groundwork for something just as important—namely, a critique of modernity from *outside* modernity. Many of today's most astute social and cultural critics seem unable to provide a perspective from beyond the boundaries of the present. They give us at most a modern critique of modernity. But by refusing to base their critiques on anything outside the dynamic of modernity itself, they place in question what is given only from within the confines of the given. Even when the "social pathologies" of modern life are superbly diagnosed or criticized, the hidden assumption is that these pathologies somehow contain their own remedies. The cure for modernity is simply—more modernity. Habermas, for one, assumes this position in his

immanent critique of modernity. His goal is to accept the basic configurations of modern life and then push for what he calls the *completion* of
the project of modernity (by which he means, among other things,
driving out a misdirected instrumental rationality and replacing it with
"communicative rationality"). Though there are advantages to this approach, there are also notable shortcomings, one of which is that virtually no attention is paid to the critical possibilities of past traditions.
Instead, such traditions are too often dismissed as merely "backward-
oriented forms of community."[14] To many critics today, the old traditions
contain nothing more than superseded values and practices which deserve to be consigned to the dustbin of history.

Needless to say, I think this is the wrong way to look at tradition.
Moreover, I believe that the error it represents is to a great extent built
into the very methodology of immanent critique. Being dialectical, an
immanent critique seeks to take the best from a given situation and
move it forward toward fulfillment. Its main interest is in those supposedly progressive elements that can be driven beyond the limitations
of their circumstances toward a higher realization. Though this method
is inherently radical, it is nevertheless hampered by one major over-
sight: it has little to say about the seemingly unprogressive elements that
have been transcended. In an immanent critique these discarded elements, including traditions, are generally thought to contain little of
value, since they have not been *aufgehoben,* that is, preserved and raised
to a higher level. But the point should not be to dismiss what has been
left behind by modernity, but to reconsider it with respect to the critical
potential it still contains.

To state my position clearly, I am not in principle opposed to an
immanent critique of modernity, though in practice such a critique has
had its problems. Nor am I arguing for a rejection of modernity, or for
some sort of return to premodernity. Rather, my point is that, while
accepting modernity *tout court,* we need to acquire more critical leverage against its most dangerous tendencies, and for this we need contact
with the otherness of tradition.

If lapsed or defeated traditions are simply ignored, or if they are
approached merely cognitively as curiosities from the past, they will lack
consequences; they will then indeed become the detritus of history some
critics claim they are. But if these traditions are brought out of obscurity
and inserted more provocatively into the present, they can have a creatively disruptive effect, because they bring with them a host of alternate

beliefs and practices whose very strangeness makes them disturbing. At the same time, many of the important substantive traditions of the past also carry with them a repertoire of critical concepts which have been occluded, suppressed, or simply forgotten by modernity. These abandoned or neglected concepts not only do not play by the prevailing rules of the game, in the sense that they do not "fit in" with what we call normativity, but they also tend to call our rules and norms into question. Hence, by regarding what is in light of what is excluded or repressed, it is possible to gain an angle of vision on modernity which cannot help but raise doubts about many of our otherwise well-protected illusions.

What we need, then, is neither more forgetting nor the kind of recovery of the past which reduces difference to sameness. Rather, we need a non-nostalgic *recherche du temps perdu* to expand and deepen the possibilities of critique. Even the best social commentators today have, I believe, greatly underestimated the critical power of memory. To be sure, what social or cultural memory brings forth often seems outmoded by the standards of modernity, which is why it is customary to label as useless or irrelevant that which is dredged up from the past. But from another point of view it is precisely the obsolescence of what memory brings forward that is valuable today, for what modernity calls historically passé often contains the very otherness we most require to broaden and deepen our perspective on modern life.

Two centuries ago, when the Enlightenment philosophes spoke of liberation, they could conceive of it in no other way than as liberation from tradition. For them, it was only after the authority of the past had been abolished that an era of freedom could begin. With this attitude the Enlightenment helped usher in modernity which *was* emancipatory when compared to the world it replaced. But modernity then brought a new set of problems as severe as those it supplanted. Now once again it seems that a kind of liberation is needed, but this time a liberation from the worst aspects of modernity *while paradoxically remaining within the framework of modernity*. To achieve this objective, a recuperation of tradition is required to lift us out of immediacy and give us greater critical leverage. To the philosophes such a conclusion would have been unthinkable, since for them tradition was almost by definition an obstacle to progress. Today, we perhaps need to look at tradition less narrowly, for if there is to be a way forward in history as the Enlightenment hoped, it will most likely come not against, but with the help of, tradition.

The "Need for Tradition" Reconsidered

Everything I have been discussing so far concerns only defunct traditions. But to recall the beginning of the chapter, there are three conditions in which traditions find themselves: they can be terminated and yet linger on as fragments, they can survive with the aid of the state or market, or they can persist on their own, but at the margins of social life.

The latter two conditions are as important as the first, and the traditions that survive within them should also be contacted. However, in contacting them one cannot experience otherness in the way it can be experienced with those traditions that have receded into the past, because extant traditions simply do not carry the same shock value. Why contact them, then? The best answer, I believe, is not the one that might be expected—viz., because they satisfy certain deeply ingrained needs for security, stability, and continuity. As I have already indicated, it is possible that today even surviving traditions cannot satisfy the needs they did in the past—and neither, probably, can anything else. We may have to accept the fact that we are now essentially "un-housed." We might continue to long for tradition, but no law of existence says this longing has to be fulfilled. Of course, for millennia it was, but this kind of fulfillment may simply no longer be available. One of the consequences of modernity is that the connection between the need to feel anchored or "at home" and the availability of tradition to satisfy this need, has been broken. The state, the market, and the culture industry have offered a variety of substitutes, but ultimately they do not seem to be adequate. Even the ability of naturally surviving traditions (which I will discuss later) to provide what Homer called "a [firm] place to stand on this earth," has been greatly weakened. Most such traditions have withdrawn into the private realm or have been pushed to the edges of social life where they maintain an uncertain existence, at best. Where they satisfy at all, they satisfy only partially, never completely.

If surviving traditions do not embody radical difference, and if they are unable to fulfill the needs they once did, then of what value are they? In my view, their chief value lies in the help they provide in addressing some of the major problems of the present age.

During the past 100 years or so—from Nietzsche and Weber to Foucault, Habermas and Lyotard—there has been general agreement among social critics as to what constitutes the central problems of modernity. They include, among other things, the problems of rationalization, commodification, and instrumentalization, the erosion of the lifeworld, the growing manipulation of consensus, the atomization of experience, and the disintegration of individual autonomy and subjectivity. Though these problems have been given different weight and emphasis by different critics, all agree that they add up to matters of serious concern for the West in the late-twentieth century. In my opinion, it is in reference to such pivotal issues of our time that the greatest value of surviving traditions lies. As I intend to show in the following chapters, surviving traditions not only help us address many of these pressing issues more satisfactorily, but also provide at least some tentative solutions to them.

In saying this, it is important to emphasize that it is not tradition *in general* that addresses or solves the problems of modernity. To understand exactly what tradition has to offer, it is necessary to assess each of the three conditions that tradition is in, since the degree to which a tradition can be rendered valuable will depend upon how it is approached in each of its particular conditions. If, for example, a tradition has been terminated, it should be approached in one way; if artificially sustained, in another way; and if naturally surviving, in yet another. In Chapter 6, I focus specifically on methods of contacting discontinued traditions through their surviving residues. In Chapter 7, I shift to a discussion of how to approach traditions manipulated by the state or market. And in Chapter 8, I discuss traditions that have persisted underground, in the private sphere, or at the fringes of society. In each case, I describe the value that I think these various traditions possess, especially in relation to the central problems of modernity.

6 Reappropriating Tradition through Its Traces

There are traditions that once existed but now exist no more. Some have vanished without a trace, while others have left behind evidence of their presence. Based on this lingering evidence, it is possible not only to contact these defunct traditions, but to bring some aspects of their otherness into the present age.

Two kinds of evidence allow inactive traditions to be discovered and engaged. The first kind might be referred to as a surviving fragment of tradition. When traditions disappear, some of their elements can continue on in bits and pieces, and can even assume lives of their own separate from the unities of which they were once a part. In such cases, the traditions pass away *as traditions,* but their traces survive in fragments of value and behavior which testify to the historical existence of something that had once flourished but is present no longer. Examples of remnants of this sort would include various provincialisms, abandoned preindustrial modes of thought and action, superseded codes of honor, archaic forms of spirituality and asceticism, precapitalist modes of work and sharing, outmoded ethical canons, and antiquated styles of human relation and interaction. All of these *parts* of tradition may seem strange or out of place, but this is only because each is a vestige of a whole way of life that has ceased to exist except for its remaining traces.

The second kind of evidence that makes it possible to contact bygone traditions is the written word. Some traditions that have been depleted or destroyed without leaving any living fragments behind can still be reached through the medium of the written record. Two types of writing provide access to these seemingly lost traditions: the work of historical or ethnographic description, and the literary text. With regard to the first, scholars, memoirists, or folklorists from the past were often aware that many of the traditions then extant were on the verge of disappearing. These individuals carefully described what they could observe about the traditions of their time, and some did so in great detail.[1] When the traditions did in fact vanish from social life, these written accounts survived intact. Most were subsequently drawn on by cultural historians who then wove still richer descriptions of the traditions and what they meant to the people who experienced them first-hand.

The other type of writing, the literary text, makes former traditions available in a more roundabout but perhaps equally effective way. Every artistically crafted work written in the past, especially in the distant past, was composed within a traditional context that was simply taken for granted. But since that context has now faded into history, literary texts have become, almost in spite of themselves, representative documents that attest to the existence of formerly active practices or beliefs. To the extent that these texts, when written, intentionally or unintentionally encoded traditions no longer present in daily life, they provide access to what would otherwise be inaccessible. Virgil's *Aeneid,* for example, or Dante's *Divine Comedy* were expressly written as works of poetry; they were not written to preserve traditions for posterity. Nonetheless, both poems contain a great amount of material regarding past traditions that are no longer embedded in *any* contemporary practices. By interpreting or "dialoguing with" literary texts such as these, one can contact inactive traditions with a unique kind of directness made possible only through language.

In the pages that follow, I will discuss both kinds of evidence of previous traditions: the kind found in surviving fragments, and the kind found in written works. I intend to describe how each might be approached, and then suggest what one might "do" with the traditions to which each type of trace refers.

1. Reclaiming the Fragment

Noncontemporaneity

A fragment of a former tradition can be either a surviving habit of mind or a surviving facet of behavior. If it is the first, it may be a mode of thinking, perceiving, or valuing which has become detached from the context that once sustained it. In its original setting the habit of mind may have had a particular place and meaning, conferred in part by the

93

network of relations in which it was ensconced. If that historical context is destroyed, remnants from it become disengaged and float free of their previous relations; they may even survive, alone and isolated, decades or generations after the demolition of their primary context. When this happens, the fragment's original meaning is often lost, and the fragment itself gets absorbed and integrated into another, that is, a contemporary register of value. One sees this in isolated parts of Europe where residues of pre-Christian religious traditions have been incorporated into Catholic rituals and ceremonies. It shows up as well among emigrant families whose Old-World frames of reference or forms of thought survive, but only by being reworked to fit New-World settings. Such processes of detachment and reassimilation occur more frequently than is generally realized. And they happen entirely apart from the calculated manipulations of the state and market, which, because they are strategically planned, are of a completely different order than what I am describing here.

A fragment of a previous tradition can also be a surviving facet of behavior, i.e., some form of activity that lingers on after the framework in which it once had significance perishes. Here, too, the detached remnant can be worked into a new framework of meaning, or be invested with a different set of values. When this occurs, old practices and patterns may continue from one generation to the next, but after a while they simply no longer mean what they originally did. For instance, activities centering around the coming of the New Year are actually enduring relics of Roman, and even more ancient traditions. As people participate in these celebrations today, they may not realize that they are unwittingly reenacting parts of traditions that have long since disappeared. Similarly, in Europe, residues of medieval folk customs and practices have persisted down to our own time, but because so many of them have been reconstituted for the tourist trade, they now signify in ways very different than they did centuries ago.[2]

Wherever fragments of either traditional mental outlooks or traditional forms of behavior survive into the present, no matter how distorted, so too do real, palpable traces of "noncontemporaneity." To my knowledge, this term was coined in the 1920s by the art historian Wilhelm Pinder who spoke, entirely within the context of art history, of the "*Gleichzeitigkeit der Ungleichzeitigen*" ("the contemporaneity of the noncontemporaneous"). Later the term was picked up and expanded by Karl Mannheim, who used it to explain the kinds of generational conflicts that emerge when people who have experienced different "forms of time" coexist at the same time. In the 1930s the concept was appropriated and expanded still further by Ernst Bloch who drew it into a Marxist framework. Bloch was concerned to show that remnants of noncontemporaneity are not merely useless pieces of debris from the past, but rather very powerful catalyzing agents that can be used in either a progressive or regressive direction. The Nazis learned how to utilize such remnants with reactionary intent, but Bloch hoped that some aspects of tradition—what he called its "nonsynchronous contradictions"—could be employed even more effectively as critical weapons to combat an unacceptable status quo.[3]

In reference to tradition, noncontemporaneity denotes something that originated in and was appropriate to an earlier era but which continues on into the present. The noncontemporaneous fragment can be relatively recent or from the more distant past, but either way there is always something disjunctive about it; it never quite fits into its new setting. Part of the reason for this lack of fit is that the fragment, almost in spite of itself, goes on signalling backward to its previous meanings even after it has been recontextualized. Though temporally cut off from the traditional whole of which it was once a part, the fragment continues to refer to its lost totality. Hence it is never just a dead possession from the past; it carries a part of the spirit of the past with it.

Many have noticed how this process works with respect to artifacts, but have failed to see that the same thing happens with noncontemporaneous habits of mind and modes of behavior. The Parthenon, for example, is a fragment of the past that has survived into the present. It is interesting to the tourist not necessarily because of its physical features, but because it conveys something about Greek sensibility in the Classical Age. The Parthenon, in its noncontemporaneity, succeeds in communicating this something even though the Classical Age itself has long since disappeared as an historical reality. Similarly, an American visitor to a Mexican village may bring back, say, a cradle from the colonial period and use it as a magazine rack. The cradle, functionally speaking, becomes a magazine holder, but it is also much more than that, since it continues to signal other messages about the nature of primitive art, Mexican folk culture, "Latin-Americanness," and the like. For the owner, or for those he may be trying to impress, there is little doubt that the cradle's primary value lies in the previous codes it still contains, not simply in its usefulness as a magazine rack.[4]

The same kind of signaling backwards occurs with regard to vestiges from traditional modes of thinking and acting. When we observe such vestiges in ourselves or others, we recall a past that is no more, but that somehow continues to live on in its referents. For instance, some forms of ethical thought and behavior are clearly antiquated by modern standards, and yet they persist in the conduct of some people as deeply felt convictions. Sometimes, especially in periods of crisis, such convictions can manifest themselves in acts of great moral heroism.[5] When this occurs, one is suddenly reminded that there are other ways to be or to live a life—ways that were strongly emphasized in the past but that have largely been lost sight of in our contemporary culture of forgetting.

In a similar vein, Max Weber, writing in the early 1890s, pointed out the persistence in German social life of outmoded aristocratic attitudes and styles of conduct. In a Germany that was becoming increasingly rationalized and industrialized, Weber believed that these traditional aristocratic ideals and modes of experience were indispensable precisely because they were noncontemporaneous. In his view, the modern world of "mechanized petrification" needed residues from the past in order not to fall into the banality of bourgeois present-mindedness. Without aristocratic notions of grace, wholeness, "inner fate," honor, and *Ritterdienst* (the ability to be dedicated to something beyond the self), life, Weber felt, would be stripped of a certain qualitative dimension which, once lost, could not be restored.[6]

In our own time, the surviving fragments of discontinued traditions are for the most part not even noticed, since they have generally been incorporated into prevailing frameworks. Once integrated, their angular or discordant aspects often get lost from view. Even fragments from once-powerful traditions become weakened and their original meanings begin to fade away. Unless this process is somehow arrested, the non-contemporaneous eventually comes to be treated as simply another facet of the contemporaneous.

The Aura of Tradition

It appears to be true, as Henri Lefebvre has argued, that we are presently experiencing a "decline of the referentials" in modern life.[7] At the very least, it seems that fewer references to the past are encountered in present-day culture, particularly in the modern city.[8] As people learn to adjust to modernity, many traditional forms of thinking and behaving disappear, and much of what does not disappear gets absorbed and recontextualized. Because the new is now more highly valued than the old, the new not only tends to replace the old, but often erases its material signs and markings. However, the obliteration of the traces of tradition has not been total by any means. The referentials may have declined but they have not disappeared, and where they survive they can still be used to evoke aspects of the past within the present. But in order to restore the past in this way, the half-hidden fragments of tradition must first of all be *noticed;* then they have to be dislodged from their secondary contexts and seen in light of their original meanings. By treating traditional fragments not as curiosities but rather as indicators of something not present, forms of life that have vanished can be imaginatively brought to mind. Just as the hunter can see in a track or a footprint an indication of an animal that had recently been present but is now absent, and just as he can visualize on the basis of the track the nature of the animal that left it, so too one can mentally re-create the past on the basis of remnants that have survived into the present.

What such remnants are able to open up if approached correctly are the cultural codes, the ambience and atmosphere, and the underlying system of meaning and relation within which the now-isolated fragment once flourished. Even though the fragments from the past have generally been overlaid with secondary elaborations, their earlier messages still reverberate. In this respect, one could say that the relation of the fragment to the whole from which it has been separated is similar to the relation which the poet Heine once observed between certain shellfish and the ocean from which they came. Though kept in a room far from their natural surroundings, the shellfish, as Heine noted, "still feel the distant movements of the sea, the ebb and flow of the tides; they still open and close, but in the midst of an alien world, their movements are misplaced and meaningless."[9]

Expressed differently, what is preserved in the fragment is what might be called the "aura" of tradition. I use this term as Walter Benjamin did when he spoke of the kind of aura a work of art possesses when it simply is what it is, i.e., when it manifests its essential character. But the character of every cultural creation is historically specific; its essence is determined partly by its social setting and partly by its temporal location. Hence, according to Benjamin, every artwork initially exists and thrives in its own proper time and space within "the domain of tradition." Whether intended or not, it also exudes something of the atmosphere of "the place where it happens to be." If it is extracted from its context—or "pry[ed] from its shell," as Benjamin says—the aura seems to dissolve, producing a "tremendous shattering of tradition."[10]

In fact, however, the aura only appears to dissolve with time; it is never completely lost. Even after a traditional object has been recontextualized, something of the aura can yet be detected. It is for this reason that antiques remain valuable: they hint at an aura that in some elusive way still surrounds them. It is also why Benjamin thinks that old photographs contain a "melancholy incomparable beauty"; they preserve intact traces of the moment in which they were taken, a moment which in itself is wholly irrecoverable. The same can be said of those fragments of thought or practice that have survived into the present, only to be enveloped by the completely different atmosphere of modernity. They continue, in spite of themselves, to suggest "a phenomenon of a distance, however close [they] may be."[11] The distance spoken of here is of course not spatial but temporal; it is the distance represented by the aura of tradition. Wherever such an aura can be felt or sensed, one comes into contact with historical otherness. The key importance of the aura is that it communicates noncontemporaneity, which is to say, it expresses something profoundly different from what is familiar or commonplace today. But the only way to grasp this otherness is to treat the fragment of tradition as a trace, and then let the trace evoke the lost totality of which it was once an integral part, and to which it still indirectly refers.

The Shock Effect of Otherness

If it is accepted that residues of noncontemporaneous thinking and acting are still extant today, and if it is agreed that these residues contain something of the aura of previous traditions, then one needs to ask what one should do with these traces of otherness.

Several answers immediately suggest themselves. First, one could try to abolish traces of otherness altogether because of the high level of discomfort they might evoke. The assumption here would be that by eliminating all references to noncontemporaneity, one would also eliminate the difference that the past represents, thereby making possible a pure, unconflicted modernity. Second, and less drastic, one could allow the traces to persist, but attempt to neutralize their effect. This might be done by so thoroughly incorporating fragments of past traditions into present structures that they would no longer be able to disturb or threaten. In this way, otherness would be reduced to sameness, difference would be subsumed into identity. Even though traces from the past would be tolerated, their primary meanings and messages would for all practical purposes be effaced. Third, one could not merely tolerate traces of noncontemporaneity, but could make a conscious and deliberate effort to preserve them intact. The main, and on the face of it, laudable goal of this approach would be to collect and cherish fragments of otherness before they disappear entirely. But it can and has happened that this drive to preserve may take an antiquarian turn, in which case the interest in the traditional remnants becomes obscurantist. In the very effort to save them, fragments from the past can become fossilized and made inconsequential. Should this occur, the residues of tradition begin to be not merely acknowledged, but revered and venerated; to the extent that this happens, these same residues tend to be kept at an excessively respectful distance, and hence not brought to bear on contemporary problems.

In contrast to these three notions of what to do with the surviving traces of otherness, I would suggest yet another option—the only one that, in my view, possesses real merit. It is one that grants that fragments from the past do survive, but accepts that for the most part they have been assimilated into the structures and frameworks of modern life. The task therefore would be to bracket them out of their present surroundings and accentuate what it is about them that is *different* from modernity. If this kind of extraction were done, noncontemporaneous traces of tradition could be seen in relation to the past from which they have come rather than in relation to the present into which they have been integrated. Aspects of tradition might then be sharply juxtaposed to contemporary forms of life in order to heighten contrasts and increase contradictions. To confront a fragment from the past, starkly and without mediation, could arouse curiosity about the fragment's original meaning and send the mind backwards, provoking memory and reflection. Momentarily, at least, part of the aura of the past would be present, delivering "its long forgotten message in surroundings utterly alien to it."[12] One of the gains of this type of radical juxtaposition would be that an historical or diachronic dimension would enter into our overly synchronous present. But more: if an awareness of tradition were brought forward in this way, it would perhaps jar or unsettle present-day securities, disturb complacencies, and put our certainties into question, since what is taken-for-granted would be seen anew in light of the past. Reevaluations of this sort could in turn lead to a certain healthy dissociation from the present, out of which might come a more critical attitude toward the generally unchallenged configurations of modern life.

This is not to say that every true perception of noncontemporaneity produces all these consequences. But it does sometimes happen that, when oppositions are highlighted or differences accentuated, a process of reverse valuations comes to the fore and gains credibility. Though I think the process of reversing valuations is necessary today, I am not suggesting that we can find in the otherness of tradition a viable *alternative* to the present, for to take such a position would be to fall into the error of traditionalism. Rather, I am suggesting that the primary value of reclaiming the traces of tradition and juxtaposing them to modernity lies in the potential of this method to shock people into clearer assessments of what is (or should be) considered normative. When the past abruptly intrudes into the present, or when the normal flow of life is disrupted by an unexpected breakthrough of otherness, the givens of modern culture become problematized.[13] By encountering radical noncontemporaneity, some might be led to scrutinize "the way things are" more carefully, or to question aspects of modernity without at the same time trying to flee into an irrecoverable past.

There is something to be said for this approach. Under the right circumstances the sudden experience of difference can shake one up and may even help to undermine a misplaced confidence in the conventional truths of the age. But the juxtapositional method has its own problems as well. For one thing, it asks tradition to perform a task opposite the one it has always performed—that is, to disturb the familiar rather than sustain it—and this reversal of functions is no easy chore. For another, if people are truly to be affected by the aura of tradition preserved in noncontemporaneous traces, they must first be able to *see* the historical otherness to which the trace refers. But to see this requires precisely the kind of background knowledge about the past that appears to be lacking today. We have a notoriously weak sense of history and an even weaker feel for the texture of earlier periods. This is why, when a trace is encountered, the aura of tradition in it is not usually seen, or if it is, it tends to be regarded exclusively from the point of view of the present. But if the noncontemporaneous is viewed through the lenses of contemporaneity, everything important about it is missed. The result is that when a fragment from the past is set in relief against the present, oppositions are not noted, tensions go unrecognized, contrasts are not

100

seen. Even incommensurabilities can be placed side by side without arousing comment. All of these difficulties make it hard to utilize the juxtapositional method effectively.

In the same regard, it cannot be forgotten that our culture is probably the most eclectic that human history has produced. Practically everything has been drawn into it and given some legitimate place, including a whole range of material from the past as well as a multiplicity of values, artifacts, and commodities manufactured in the present. When this much variety exists simultaneously, nothing shocks anymore. Even the most profound contradictions within everyday life are not experienced as contradictions, and hence the jarring effect hoped for by the juxtapositional method becomes difficult to attain.

There is, however, another way to contact discontinued traditions which does not depend upon the effectiveness of stark juxtaposition. This second approach is one which seeks to *evoke* an awareness of otherness rather than to try and jolt one into recognizing it.

2. Dialoguing with Tradition

The Nature of Dialogue

Earlier in this chapter I spoke of writing as a second mode of access to bygone traditions, and more particularly of two kinds of writing especially helpful in this regard: historical-ethnographic works and literary texts. With respect to the first, I pointed out that one can become acquainted with traditions that have disappeared by means of written accounts that describe what they were once like. In France, for example, a long-standing tradition of rural gatherings known as the *veillées* completely vanished from the countryside by the early twentieth century. Nevertheless, thanks to the careful descriptions of Eugen Weber and others, a reader can come to know this "lost" tradition fairly intimately, even without having observed or participated in it.[14] The values the *veillées* manifested, the ways of life they embodied, can therefore still be contacted, though of course, as with all such writings, only in a second-hand way.

As for the literary text—which I will focus on exclusively in the following pages—it too is able to convey something of the noncontemporaneity of the past, but in a different manner than simply through factual knowledge. Whenever a text is handed down from one age to the next, it unavoidably carries with it traces of historical otherness. Especially if a work remains unaltered in the process of transmission, it continues to communicate in print exactly what it expressed originally. In this respect, reading such a work gives one direct acquaintance with a particular moment in the past. In fact, by encountering tradition linguistically in this fashion one may be able to experience it less obliquely than in surviving fragments of belief or practice. In the latter case, one has imaginatively to reconstruct the aura of tradition from the trace, whereas in a text tradition is able to express itself directly and forthrightly on its own terms.

The notion that a text can provide immediate access to tradition has been elaborated most thoroughly by Hans-Georg Gadamer. Texts, Gadamer correctly points out, are "permanently fixed expressions of life."[15] If they come from the past, they capture and crystallize not tradition as such but a certain moment in the tradition. That moment is etched into the text and then passed down exactly as it was, with the same sentences, statements, and meanings that were there at the instant it was written. In reading such a work one is able to experience the simultaneity of a past moment and a present one. Another world, another time, is thereby opened up within the context of the present. This gives a reader a kind of familiarity with and involvement in the otherness of tradition that is not obtainable in quite the same way through contact with the fragment. For this reason, the directness made possible by language permits one to experience, at least temporarily, the same dimension of meaning that one's distant ancestors were acquainted with on a daily basis.[16]

Gadamer appears correct in arguing that elements of tradition are present in texts as well as in language itself.[17] But how does one make contact with or engage these elements? Gadamer's answer is: by means of dialogue. It is worth reviewing what Gadamer says about the nature of dialogue, since he offers useful suggestions as to how one might establish a relationship to those traditions which, though they remain alive in texts, have largely disappeared as social beliefs or practices.

When two people speak not *to* but *with* one another, when they converse openly and in good faith, they can be said to be "in dialogue." For a true dialogue to occur there must be, first of all, an acknowledgment of the legitimacy of the other in the conversation. It must be assumed that one's interlocutor is an autonomous individual who is on a roughly equal footing, and who consequently has a right to his or her own opinions, even if they greatly differ from one's own. Second, each party must be willing to be honest and straightforward with the other, ready to question and be questioned without reservation. And third, each must be willing to truly *listen* to the other, to fully internalize the other's views, and hence to accept the possibility that one might have to change one's mind (or even change one's life) as a result of the conversation.

In a dialogic situation of this kind, two individuals engage one another as subjects who try to come to an understanding on an issue. This appears to be something different than dialoguing with a tradition as embodied, say, in a text, for a dialogue with a tradition is an encounter not between two subjects, but between a subject (the reader) and some object (the inscription of the tradition in language). According to Gadamer, however, a genuine dialogue between a reader and a text is possible because the medium of language encompasses and interpenetrates both, thereby setting up at least the minimum conditions for authentic communication. Beyond this, the following conditions would have to be met for real dialogue with textually inscribed traditions to take place.

To begin with, the text would have to be regarded as a subject in its own right, just as a person would be, with its own autonomy and its own point of view. When a text is treated in this way, the subject that speaks is not the author who wrote the text but the *text itself,* since every work expresses a wealth of meanings that go beyond the author's explicit intentions. Likewise, if a text happens to contain radically noncontemporaneous values or attitudes, these too would have to be granted a legitimacy of their own. Usually that which seems fundamentally *unlike* what we are used to is framed as something negative, but this response would have to be rejected. As in any genuine conversation, present-minded value judgments regarding what is right or wrong, true or false, would have to be suspended so that the text can say what it has to say without obstruction.

In addition, the text's otherness, including the alterity of the tradition it expresses, would have to be not merely accepted but sincerely respected for what it is. This means that one would have to be completely open to the text, and willing to listen attentively to its messages in order fully to hear what it has to convey. True listening is not passive but active. It connects one in an especially intimate way to that which one hears, forging a bond of "belongingness" (*Zugehörigkeit*) based on the ability to "listen" (*zuhören*) carefully and creatively.[18] Finally, beyond listening, the reader of the text would have to be able to "go over" to the spirit of the work, to abandon him or herself to its deepest meanings, and to try sincerely to understand them from the inside. This abandonment need only be temporary, and it may be primarily intellectual. But for Gadamer, authentic listening and understanding require mental or emotional empathy, though not to such an extent that one loses sight of one's own principles and is unable to gain them back again.

Put differently, the main requirement for establishing a dialogue with a text is the same one needed for establishing a dialogue with another person, namely, that the work be treated as a "thou" instead of an "it." When a text is approached in this manner, it reveals itself unreservedly; it gives up and gives over the elements of tradition locked within it. But in approaching a text as a "thou," an individual must not only be willing to bracket his prejudices and biases as much as possible in order to hear what the text has to say; he must also grant that the work could contain truths that have a greater validity than one's own. In Gadamer's words, one must be ready to recognize "the full value of what is alien and opposed."[19] If it is clear that the traditional text speaks a truth that is perhaps unpleasant but nonetheless incontrovertible, then the individual must be willing to let that truth prevail against him. In other words, he must alter or even abandon his own views in light of what he has learned from his dialogue with tradition.[20] Just as any reader should feel free to interrogate a text that comes from the past by asking any question that seems appropriate, so too he should allow the text to interrogate *him*. If this happened, the honest reciprocity and mutuality of the dialogue would come fully into its own. Something from the text would be released, but by the same token a number of contemporary certainties would surely also have to be relinquished. Hence the authentic dialogue requires a certain amount of risk. The individual who engages in a dialogue with tradition has to be willing to place his beliefs and assumptions in jeopardy in order to permit the outlook of the past to make its own claim on him.

The point of the process I have been describing is neither to embrace the traditions contained in texts so totally that one tries simply to repeat or relive them, nor to collapse the past into the present in order to, as Nietzsche put it, reduce something strange to something familiar.[21] The first option would lead to historical obscurantism or mindless traditionalism, and the second to a diminution of the power of the past and a refusal to acknowledge, let alone listen to, the past's noncontemporaneous messages. Both of these alternatives are unacceptable, but between them lies the middle path of dialogue. In a true dialogue with tradition, one stays firmly planted in the present while asking difficult questions of the tradition and allowing tradition to ask difficult questions in return. In the process of being interrogated, tradition is interpreted; by being interpreted it is brought into the present where it can become an active force.

The Limitations of Dialogue

When dialogue works, a "fusion of horizons" takes place in which the noncontemporaneous is drawn into the contemporaneous and made a vital part of everyday life.[22] For this reason, the effects produced by a dialogue with tradition are quite different than the effects produced by juxtaposition. When traditional traces are successfully juxtaposed to modernity, the result is an experience of tension and contrast. In a dialogue, however, the results are more amicable, since the goal is to reach an accord with tradition, not heighten contradictions. Moreover, a dialogue fosters genuine interest in discovering and releasing the truths hidden within eclipsed traditions, since in a dialogue it is not sufficient to use the power of otherness simply to jolt one out of complacencies. Compared to the method of juxtaposition, the method of dialogue appears to be a gentler, and perhaps in the end more effective, way to gain access to the past.

Still, a number of difficulties accompany the dialogic approach. By treating past traditions as things that are knowable only linguistically, there is the danger of reducing tradition to words and texts, or of confusing the medium through which tradition is conveyed with tradition itself. Gadamer at times seems to fall into this error when he says that tradition is "linguistic in character," or that the "mode of being of tradition . . . is language."[23] The notion that most (Gadamer would say *all*) of our experiences today are mediated by language may be accurate, but this does not mean that tradition is inseparable from language. There are traditions that continue to exist outside of words and texts and which consequently never become formally articulated or enter the realm of written documents.[24] By making language absolute, Gadamer seems unable to accept that this could happen. Instead, he often slips into what his critics have called the idealism of linguisticality, that is, he makes language not merely a conduit of tradition, but its constituent element.[25]

Similarly, Gadamer exaggerates the extent to which we still live within the flow of tradition. Nowhere in his work has he come to terms with the erosion of traditional values and continuities that has occurred in the nineteenth and twentieth centuries. Without a sound understanding of the ruptures and breakdowns that have taken place in social reality, Gadamer is unable to grasp the loss of connection with the past which is now an inescapable fact of modern life. His presumption that there exists an unbroken continuum of meaning linking the past to the present may be valid for his own discipline of philosophy, but it does not ring true when applied to other areas of life.

Finally, the success of Gadamer's approach depends on an individual's willingness and ability to conduct a dialogue with tradition. But this capacity to dialogue may itself be eroding along with much else. For a meaningful conversation with tradition to occur, people would need to be receptive to the truth claims of tradition. They would have to possess a powerful listening ability in order to hear traditions speak. If a tradition speaks but cannot be heard, everything it strains to convey would be missed. It is at least arguable that we are experiencing today a declining ability to hear, and to respond to what we hear, due to the predominance of one-way communication (film, TV, videos, etc.), and to the drying up of a public sphere founded on dialogue and discourse.[26] If there is a thinning out of dialogic capacities, and with it the loss of an ability to truly listen, a conversation with tradition would become impossible. The modern individual would be tone deaf to the voice of historical otherness; he would be able to hear, even in what is different, only what is the same.

This chapter has focused on how to contact inactive traditions and what to do with them once contact has been made. However, not all traditions have faded into the past, and therefore not all of them need to be rescued by the methods discussed here. Some traditions have continued on into the present, though often only because they have been sustained artificially. In order to reach out to these traditions, another approach is needed, one which, in the following chapter, I refer to as the genealogical method.

7 Subversive Genealogy

The Refunctioning of Tradition

We have seen how traditions can die or be extinguished and yet leave behind traces. Traditions can also survive from the past into the present, *not* because of the efforts of adherents (i.e., their will, persistence, or sheer stubbornness in believing that some tradition or other is worth preserving), but rather because of the calculated strategies of support coming from outside agencies such as the state or market.

When external agencies "save" traditions, they do not do so out of feelings of magnanimity, or because traditions are beautiful in themselves. They do so because some traditions can be useful in the pursuit of political or economic goals, such as state legitimation or corporate profit. Whenever a tradition is either appropriated in its entirety or mined for usable bits and pieces, it is invariably turned in directions that are different than, and often directly contrary to, those for which it was originally intended. For this reason, it would not be unfair to say that the price paid for artificially sustaining all or parts of any particular tradition is the misrepresentation, if not wholesale falsification, of that tradition.

Generally speaking, a misrepresentation can take one of two forms: an original tradition can simply be revised, or it can be radically transformed. If a tradition is revised, or "made over" (to use, appropriately, the language of cosmetology), it is touched up, enhanced, or glamorized, and thereby made more attractive for whatever purposes the state or market may want to use it. But if a tradition is transformed, it is either turned inside out in order to extract the material that seems useful, or it is converted into a mere facsimile of the original—but a facsimile close enough to what it imitates to suggest something of the tradition's original aura. Regardless of whether the state or market transforms or merely revises a tradition, the only reason for engaging in such an effort in the first place is to turn the tradition toward some new end or purpose. This is why it is rarely sufficient simply to prop up a tradition. A tradition usually has to be "refunctioned" as well—which is to say, it has to be lifted out of its previous setting, reconceptualized, and invested with meanings different from those it carried earlier.

The term "refunctioning" (*Umfunktionierung*), like the term noncontemporaneity, is of relatively recent origin. It was first used, with entirely radical connotations, by Bertolt Brecht, Ernst Bloch, and other Marxist intellectuals in the Germany of the 1920s. At that time, the word referred to a process of refashioning bourgeois values in such a way as to use them against their initial intention. More precisely, *Umfunktionierung* meant extracting and rearranging elements from within the capitalist system in order to set them against capitalism itself, a process Bloch referred to as salvaging "that which is true in false consciousness."[1] As it turned out, however, the real masters of the art of refunctioning were not Weimar's left-wing intellectuals but the modern state and the modern economy. And the greatest successes of refunctioning have not been those that subverted bourgeois values, but those that transformed many of the old traditions, forcing them to serve ends for which they were not initially intended.

There are at least two types of refunctioning. The first takes hold not of a whole tradition but of some extractable part or "slice" of a tradition, and then sustains that part while affixing to it new messages and meanings. The second type perpetuates a whole tradition, but only after it has been invested with new layers of signification and given new social tasks to perform. Beneath the surface differences between these two types of refunctioning is the common element of premeditation. Both are based on a manipulative utilization of tradition in order to turn it to some particular advantage. This purposive, calculative dimension makes the refunctioning practiced by the state or market entirely unlike the accidental or inadvertent refunctioning discussed in the last chapter.[2]

When Weimar's leftist intellectuals spoke of *Umfunktionierung*, they usually had the first type in mind. Mainly they wanted to perpetuate only parts of old traditions by regrouping them in new contexts. As Benjamin expressed it, the idea was to isolate certain facets of tradition, detach them from their organic settings, and then recombine them (as in a montage) in such a way as to create new constellations of meaning. These new constellations, it was assumed, would be produced *in the present,* and not simply transported wholesale from the past into the present.[3] Of course, for Benjamin and the others, the primary reason to engage in this sort of refunctioning was to deepen revolutionary consciousness with an eye toward initiating fundamental social change.

When one turns to present-day modes of refunctioning practiced by the state and the market, it is clear that both types of refunctioning are in evidence: the refunctioning of whole traditions and the refunctioning of only those parts that appear serviceable. Now, however, both types are specifically and unambiguously directed toward *non*disruptive ends. If any distinction is to be made, it is perhaps that a statist refunctioning focuses on reworking whole traditions which it instrumentalizes, while the market focuses on reworking slices of tradition which it commodifies.

For example, as I indicated in an earlier chapter, the modern state refunctions, first, by assembling under its jurisdiction numerous local, regional, or community traditions and loyalties, many of which may have existed prepolitically for generations. Second, it tries to politicize or nationalize these traditions by shaping them in such a way as to place the state at the center of these diffuse loyalties. Third, if and when this goal is achieved, the state then proceeds to encode these now "statist" traditions in several ways: by embodying them in signs and symbols (the flag, national monuments, and the like) which help evoke certain sentiments associated with the newly politicized traditions; by incorporating them into state-sponsored rituals, liturgies, and national commemorations; or by translating them into official political discourses, slogans, and grand narratives about the triumphal history of the state or its unique place in time. Last, with this much accomplished, the state is then able to promote its nationalized traditions by institutionalizing them in the legal and educational systems, and thereby commit the full weight of its authority to the task of keeping them alive and operative. Many traditions have survived into the present only because of this kind of outside help provided by the state.

The market obviously also refunctions tradition, but it does so in a different way. To begin with, it seizes upon various traditions or parts of tradition which appear to be commercially useful, and then associatively relates them to salable objects. By such means, traditions are perpetuated, but mainly in connection with commodities, and often in disfigured form. Disney Productions, for instance, appropriated and transposed into film a number of centuries-old European folk and fairy tales.

Some of the aura of these premodern tales was kept, but much else was reworked, cleaned up, and turned into a "Disney version" of the original traditions.[4] Once the Disney version existed, it was easily and quickly commodified. Eventually a host of products were created, each designed to recall some motif or character from the folk traditions. By the 1980s, these products, along with two Disney theme parks, were generating billions of dollars a year. But the folk and fairy tales that were the source of such profits were not the same ones that existed long ago, since the very elements that were retained were also transformed. In this case, as in others, the market is inclined to preserve traditions only at the cost of refunctioning them.

It is important to note that in both the statist and market refunctionings, something happens that bears little resemblance to the changes that generally affect traditions in the normal process of transmission. Typically, when a tradition is handed down from one generation to the next, it undergoes slight refinements as some small part of the tradition is discarded and some new element is added on. These modifications are often so minor that each generation may believe it is receiving a tradition intact and is passing it along unchanged. But where a process of *Umfunktionierung* is underway, a tradition is altered far more drastically, for it is not simply modified to fit new circumstances, but is deliberately altered to extract from it some political or economic benefit. A refunctioning, then, produces extreme change in a tradition. At times it even reconstitutes what it works over, thereby moving a tradition well beyond, and often against, the ends it had previously served.

The Real and the Represented

Whenever large-scale refunctionings take place in a society, two major problems become evident. The first is that in every refunctioning, authentic elements from actual traditions get mixed up with artificial elements added by the state or market. For instance, a state might retain the form of a tradition it appropriates, but strip it of its original context, suffuse it with another set of messages, and then promote it as an authentic tradition. Or the reverse could happen: an advertising agency might find it useful to seize upon the content of a tradition, including the sentiments and emotions it evokes, but separate this content from the forms that were once integral to it. Should consumers identify themselves with certain affective meanings associated with the original tradition, they would subtly be drawn into an identity with artificially created forms which may have little to do with the traditions that actually existed in the past.

If one wanted to develop a critique of this kind of refunctioning, how would it be done? One possibility would be to try to "liberate" the authentic elements of tradition from the spurious ones, not necessarily because the authentic elements are "better," but because they have been falsified and misused. If these original elements could be seen again as they once were, they would perhaps raise important questions about the political and economic configurations that twisted and distorted them. It is at least conceivable that the whole issue of how legitimate the refunctioning was in the first place would be put on the table for discussion. If this issue is not raised, refunctioned traditions can easily be passed on as authentic. In time, their fabricated nature would not be noticed and everything about them that is contrived would begin to be viewed as natural. After three or four transmissions, people would know only what is counterfeit and not what is original. More important, they would eventually come to treat the counterfeit *as* the original, and this in itself would represent a triumph of statist and marketing strategies.

Here, embedded in the very language I have just employed, is the first problem to which I referred above. When the reworking of traditions becomes pervasive, how is one to determine what part of a tradition is original and what part is manufactured? What criteria is one supposed to use to distinguish a "real" tradition from one that looks real, but is in fact only a facsimile? If a manipulated or reformed tradition is embraced by most people as the genuine article, does it then become genuine simply because it is thought to be so? These questions indicate that we may no longer be able to speak with the same confidence as our ancestors about what is real and what is not. The boundaries separating simulation from reality, the authentic from the inauthentic, even the true from the false, are simply not as clearly demarcated as they once were. It would be impossible to try and explore here all the reasons why many of the old certainties seem to be slipping away. In part it surely has to do with the ascendancy of advertising and the electronic media, which have made it harder than ever to distinguish the actual from the illusory, or even true information from disinformation. But probably a more significant cause has been the increasingly abstract nature of modern social life. In contrast to a half-century or more ago, daily existence has been saturated by a profusion of signs, codes, and images which might once have been

111

labeled "unreal," but which are now received and accepted as a normal part of social reality. To people who deal regularly with screen images, micro-dots, and computer models, the previously useful distinction between so-called material reality on the one hand, and an abstract world of signs and symbols on the other, no longer seems valid. Indeed, some commentators have argued that, for the modern individual, signs and symbols are even more real than the realm of matter since they constitute most of what we experience in everyday life.[5] If these observations about contemporary experience carry any weight at all, they would help explain why the "reality" of a tradition, like the reality of much else that surrounds us, may not be as easy to discern as it was in the past.

The entire issue of what is or is not real is complicated by a second and related problem, namely the problem of images. As I have already pointed out, both the state and the market have tried to link traditions with images. The purpose in doing this is to associate the aura of a tradition with the signalling power of an image so that in acquiring the image, people will feel that they have at the same time acquired the tradition. On the face of it, this process seems to resemble the one I described in Chapter 4, where a primordial need for rootedness, stability, and continuity was transmuted into a need for tradition. Throughout human history people have tried to satisfy their deepest primordial needs by leaning on the traditions that were always at hand. In the process, the need for tradition appears to have become a substitute for the need for rootedness, continuity, and the like. Over the centuries, the difference between the two needs probably all but vanished as the first fused with the second, disappeared into it, and eventually became indistinguishable from it.

It would seem that the identical thing happens in the way images can be made to substitute for traditions. In fact, however, the two processes are very different, for images can never really replace traditions; they can only refer to them. This distinction can be made clearer by calling the first kind of substitution (a tradition for a deeper need) a "displacement," and the second kind (an image for a tradition) a "representation." In a displacement, one thing stands *in* for another, while in a representation one thing merely stands for another. The difference the preposition makes is significant. A representation is always something *other than* the thing to which it refers. An image, for example, can allude to a real tradition but it can never be a tradition. Of course, an awareness of this difference is what manipulators of images would like to prevent. Their basic aim is to convince people that in, say, the images of a television commercial, a real displacement occurs—i.e., that an image actually becomes the equivalent of a tradition. If this were indeed what happens, then in possessing the image one would possess the tradition as well. But such a displacement cannot occur with images, since they contain, at best, only a *relation* to tradition, not tradition itself. If this simple point is blurred or forgotten, it is easy to seek in images what can never be found there. In the last analysis, to buy, or buy into, an image and expect to find a tradition is to set oneself up for disappointment.

Where, then, does all this leave us? If, thanks to the machinations of the state and market, we have images of traditions, pseudotraditions, made-over traditions, or counterfeit traditions, what attitude should we take toward this mass of material? My suggestion is that as a start we try to dismantle surviving but refunctioned traditions in order to understand which elements authentically come from the past, and which were inserted in the present with specifically manipulative ends in mind. Despite the linguistic slipperiness of such terms, I think it is still possible to separate what is real and original within a tradition from what is fake and contrived. However refunctioned a tradition may be, it nonetheless contains flecks of authenticity which need to be seen again in a new light. But in order both to glimpse these authentic elements and extract from them whatever critical power they may possess, it would be necessary to distance them from the present-day contexts into which they have been assimilated. Two methods, the deconstructive and the genealogical, seem to offer different ways to break down and reconceptualize particular aspects of refunctioned traditions. In the following pages I will examine the strengths and weaknesses of each of these methods.

The Deconstructive Method

If it can be said that deconstruction as it is presently understood originated with Derrida, then it did not begin as a full-fledged method, but only as a mode of analysis or "une stratégie générale."[6] Moreover, at first, deconstruction was an interpretive strategy only within the field of philosophy. As initially conceived, its goal was to uncover the "metaphysics of presence" allegedly inherent in Western thought since the time of the Greeks. But in short order Derrida turned his analysis to the realm of literature, an approach enthusiastically embraced by a host of literary critics, among them a large number of Americans. These critics gradually transformed Derrida's "general strategy" into a literary method replete with interpretive procedures which could be applied to any and every kind of literary work.

Today, twenty-five years after the publication of Derrida's early work, deconstruction has become a method of reading texts in such a way as to "decenter" them. To decenter a text is to uncover and elaborate the differences between its overt and covert meanings, or between what the text says and what it actually means. At the same time, deconstruction also focuses on, and tries to subvert, binary oppositions. These oppositions (presence/absence, essential/inessential, writing/speaking, etc.) are shown always to privilege one term over the other—in the examples mentioned here, the first over the second. Deconstruction strives to undermine this privileging by undoing each term and then resituating it in relation to the other. The result, invariably, is a demonstration that the favored term actually depends on the slighted one for its status and importance, because the slighted term provides the "condition of possibility" that allows the favored term to be dominant. Despite this reversal of emphasis, the deconstructive method does not try to abolish the binary oppositions with which it started. It does not, for example, attempt to collapse the first term into the second, but instead retains both while simultaneously repositioning them so that neither carries the same meaning it did previously.[7] In other words, binary oppositions are undone, but then re-created so as to keep and yet subvert the old assumptions that produced them in the first place. The point of this sometimes complicated exercise is to show that there are no "natural" meanings to a work, but rather that every meaning is arbitrary. To deconstructionists, the putative "truth" a poem or novel is said to possess at any given moment is always conventionally determined. And yet behind every conventional interpretation of what is true, there are thought to be innumerable other possible truths, each in its own way as valid (or invalid) as the dominant one.

Although deconstruction as a method has generally focused on the careful analysis of literary and philosophical texts, some attempts have been made to move it out of this realm and into the arena of social and political criticism.[8] With this move, one might think that the deconstructive method would be useful in critically approaching those traditions that have been refunctioned by the state or market. In some respects it is useful, particularly in the way it questions givens, breaks

114

down apparent unities into their constituent parts, and shows how marginalized social elements set up the conditions of possibility that allow the dominant ones to flourish. Beyond this, however, the deconstructive method has a number of shortcomings which make it less helpful than one might expect. Two are worth noting here.

The first shortcoming is that although deconstruction can indicate how wholes are put together and how they can be dismantled, it does not presume to pass judgment on either the wholes or the component parts. As Derrida has put it, value is "undecidable." There is nothing better about the parts than the whole. Nor is there any reason to cherish supposedly "good" traditional elements as opposed to the "bad" artifice of the dominant forms. From the deconstructive point of view, every given is merely an improvised construct, but so too is every tradition drawn into the given, for traditions are themselves only constructs made up of still other traditional elements, and so on, *ad infinitum*. In this swirl of continuous appropriation and reappropriation, it is impossible to assign value to any particular part at the expense of any other part. Hence, despite the often radical tone of its language ("subversion," "unmasking," "erasure," etc.), deconstruction never calls for the *replacement* of one set of values with another. It merely calls for a proliferation of possible meanings, or the opening up of hidden meanings, but it refuses to say that any meaning is better than, or superior to, any other. Thus, because it has no objections to the process of refunctioning itself, deconstruction appears unable to provide the leverage needed critically to assess statist or market refunctionings. It is perhaps not surprising, then, that without an operative set of values with which to work, so much deconstructive criticism has ended in play: the play of signification, the play on words, punning, double and triple entendre, and numerous ironic reversals and inversions that have now become a familiar part of the deconstructionist repertoire.[9]

The second shortcoming of deconstruction—at least as far as its usefulness for a critique of refunctioned traditions is concerned—is just as serious. It has to do with the way deconstruction tends to neglect or deemphasize the temporal dimension. In general, the deconstructive method is not historically oriented. It has very little interest in going back in time to explain the temporal unfolding of elements that constitute today's givens. But it may be that to truly understand what refunctioning is and how it works, it is necessary to take history into account. Because deconstruction does not do so, or does so very inadequately, it seems incapable of dealing with the most important issues of sequence and duration. When the deconstructive method is applied to some contemporary instance of refunctioning—an instance in which both the process of refunctioning itself and the material refunctioned come entirely from the present—it can provide valuable insights. But when deconstruction tries to deal with the refunctioning of traditions, the elements involved are quite different. In this case, the *process* of refunctioning is something that happens in the present, while the *material* refunctioned comes from the past. New problems arise when the temporal dimension is added, since now the issue is not just how recombinations as such occur, but how nonsynchronous combinations are created.

With this in mind, what appears to be needed is a special type of deconstruction—a *genealogical* deconstruction—which would dismantle diachronically rather than synchronically. It would show how the state and market purposely sustain traditions that stem from different historical periods, and how they revise or revamp these traditions in the process of perpetuating them. By starting with the actuality of refunctioned traditions, this method would trace layer by layer the constituent elements of these traditions back through time, and in so doing, lay the groundwork for a different kind of subversion than that proposed by Derridean deconstruction. In the following section, I will define what I mean by the genealogical method, and then describe some of the advantages this approach holds for a critique of refunctioned traditions.

"Constructive Sabotage"

It may seem odd to speak of genealogy as subversive, for this is not the role it has played historically. From earliest times genealogy has served primarily conservative ends. In ancient Near Eastern societies, for example, dynastic genealogies (King Lists) were used to legitimize established political authority.[10] In Greece, aristocratic families justified their high position with reference to their ancestral pedigrees. The *geneos* to which one belonged established one's identity; to have no reputable genealogy was to have no status and therefore to hardly exist at all.[11] Likewise, in medieval Europe the nobility relied heavily on genealogical claims to justify privilege. The further back one could trace a family lineage—ideally back to the Age of Charlemagne, if possible—the more secure was one's place at the top of social or political hierarchies.[12]

116

But accompanying the conservative and stabilizing effects of genealogy there has always been an awareness, at least on the part of a few, that genealogy can also be used against power. In the right hands it can reveal an embarrassing history of crime and rapaciousness which the established authorities would prefer to hide from view. Or it can uncover what Nietzsche called the *pudenda origio,* the "shameful origin" of existing values and institutions which, when known, would discredit both them and the power structures they support. (Hobbes indicated the danger inherent in genealogy when, in his *Leviathan,* he wrote that "there is scarcely a commonwealth in the world whose beginnings can in conscience be justified." And Kant, too, remarked that the question of origin can easily "threaten the state with danger if asked with too much sophistication."[13]) Yet perhaps Nietzsche more than anyone else saw the radical possibilities of genealogy. As a critic of his age he often relied on the genealogical method to undermine dominant values. However, since Nietzsche believed that one of the central problems of his time was the tyranny of the past over the present, he used genealogy in a different way than I am suggesting here. Primarily he employed it to assault tradition and break its grip on modern thought, for he was sure that only when the heavy hand of the past had been removed could the present come into its own, or the future be authorized.[14]

The kind of subversive genealogy I have in mind would not, like Nietzsche's, try to destroy the past's hold on the present, but rather destroy the present's hold on the past. Today the oppressiveness of tradition is not our problem. We are not victims of the past and are not straitjacketed by past determinations. Instead, the danger lies more with the exploitative refunctioning of tradition, particularly in the political and economic spheres. A subversive genealogy in the context of the present would address this issue, first, by analyzing what is closest at hand—i.e., the instrumentalized and commodified traditions that surround us—and would then move backward in time in order to chart their origin and development. It would do this by breaking down contemporary refunctionings into their parts, showing what role each part now plays and what new meanings have been assigned to each artificially sustained tradition. This amounts to the synchronic first step of a subversive genealogy. But second, this kind of genealogy would need to shift into a diachronic dimension by tracing each reworked facet of a tradition back in time in order to locate the point where an apparently authentic tradition, or part of one, became inauthentic: the point, that is, where it began to be pulled from its context and refunctioned politically or economically.

A "regressive" method such as this may be able to indicate at least three things: (1) what a tradition was *originally* at the time of its emergence; (2) what it became *historically* as it unfolded through a chain of transmissions; and (3) what it became *after* it was refunctioned. There is no satisfactory way to understand these three dimensions or the relations between them except by following traditions back, in reverse sequence, from the immediate present to the distant past. The result of this kind of work should be a greater comprehension of how power, by invisible strategies of conversion, is able to appropriate and transform what it needs from the past. At the same time, it should reveal the extent to which the authority of artificially sustained traditions is falsely acquired, and how much of what we now take to be tradition is not at all what tradition has been originally or historically.[15]

Here, however, something important should be noted. When a tradition is preserved but revamped, many of its earlier meanings are dispensed with and new meanings superimposed. But these earlier meanings often linger on and can still be perceived in the refunctioned tradition. Sometimes these older meanings persist accidentally, as mere echoes or after-effects of what they once were. But frequently they continue on because they are intentionally preserved. At times, the state or market finds value in some previous traditional meaning, not necessarily because the meaning itself is so significant, but because it possesses a particular kind of aura which could prove useful in selling or legitimizing something or other. A traditional aura can be especially potent when it contains a certain "charge" or "energy" which, if tapped successfully, can evoke a variety of feelings and sentiments that may be exploited for commercial or political ends. Modern marketing experts, for example, have made an art of capitalizing on the "charge" of tradition in such a way as to convert it into a desire for specific products identified with the aura. Twentieth-century political ideologues have developed similar techniques. The Nazis were especially adept at playing on emotional associations rooted in tradition. Concepts such as *Volk* or *Gemeinschaft,* both of which carried rich historical meanings, were utilized by the state apparatus in such a manner as to preserve their traditional resonances (suggesting warmth, community, belongingness), but only in order to refunction them in a National Socialist direction.[16]

The "energy" I am talking about might be called a *surplus energy,* that

118

is, an excess of meaning and affect coming from the past and continuing into the present. This surplus is valuable to the state and market for the reasons I have already mentioned. But neither the state nor the market can possibly utilize all of this surplus; they need only that part which is functionally useful. This turns out to be a relatively small portion of the total expenditure of meaning a tradition puts forth from the time of its origin to the time that it becomes refunctioned. The excess *beyond* this usable portion nevertheless continues to linger on in the form of mnemonic traces which preserve those still-important meanings and messages which seem dysfunctional in the present situation.

The task of a subversive genealogy in this regard would be to call attention to these surpluses of meaning and then to "unconceal" them. Within even artificially sustained traditions, there are unstated values and meanings (always the ones that shoot beyond mere utility) that can be released. These hidden or suppressed elements call into question the present-day uses of tradition simply by recalling earlier meanings lodged within the *same* tradition. In this respect, a subversive genealogy produces a kind of counter-memory which rehabilitates what has been excluded. Bloch had just this sort of rehabilitation in mind when he spoke of an "unclaimed heritage" that needs to be repossessed.[17] It would appear that the kind of subversive genealogy I have been describing here would be equipped to uncover and liberate this heritage. To do this would of course be no easy undertaking. It would require a great deal of knowledge and interpretive skill on the part of the subversive genealogist. It would also require that those who encounter a genealogical analysis be steeped in enough history to fully grasp the multiplicity of meanings being recuperated. It may be that neither of these requirements can be met today, particularly if it is true, as many have argued, that we live in a thoroughly dehistoricized postmodern condition.

Despite these problems, a subversive genealogy remains perhaps the best way to approach existing but artificially sustained traditions. It is not, however, the best way to approach naturally surviving but marginalized traditions, since these have not been refunctioned and do not need to be deconstructed. Because these naturally surviving traditions are so different from manipulated ones, they call for a different kind of contact. What this mode of contact is and how it can be achieved is the subject of the following chapter.

8   The Tactics of Tradition

Naturally Surviving Traditions

Despite the numerous assaults on tradition in the West since the seventeenth century, some traditions have managed to survive more or less intact. These traditions fall into the last of the three categories I have been describing, namely, those that have continued to exist *on their own terms,* entirely apart from the help or support of outside agencies. (I have been calling traditions such as these "naturally surviving" traditions, but I mean nothing Darwinian by this term. I mean only that there are traditions that persist not because they have been recast from without, but because they have been kept alive and carried forward from within, due to the will and determination of their adherents.)

In the following pages I will examine these naturally enduring traditions to see why they have been able to survive, and to discuss some ways in which to respond to them. With regard to the other types of traditions treated earlier—the discontinued and refunctioned traditions—one's response to them must be primarily intellectual. However, with surviving autonomous traditions, one can respond either in an intellectual or in a practical way. Because such traditions are still extant, one has the choice to become directly and actively involved with them in a manner that is not possible when traditions exist only in fragments, or when they have been reconstituted as statist symbols or commercial images.

How is it that some traditions have persevered in spite of the great resistance shown to them during the past three or four centuries? In some cases survival has been due to pure inertia; a tradition may build up enough force or persistence to continue on even after it has outlived the conditions that once sustained it. More often, however, a tradition survives because it fulfills some need which would not otherwise be satisfied. A great many familial and communal traditions have endured because they are attentive to particular human wants and desires which are simply not addressed elsewhere. Likewise, a basic need for collective identity helps account for the persistence of certain social or cultural traditions. In sixteenth- and seventeenth-century Europe, the tiny Catholic enclaves which remained intact within Protestant areas maintained their *esprit de corps* by preserving their cultural and religious traditions with special tenacity; the same was true of Protestants within Catholic areas. Similarly, in the twentieth century, the unwanted presence of the Soviet Union in Eastern Europe after World War II fostered the preservation of many national traditions which under normal circumstances might have faded in importance. In Poland and Czechoslovakia, for example, historical traditions once looked upon as insignificant or outmoded were conscientiously preserved, because they helped maintain a sense of national identity in the face of policies that seemed likely to obliterate such identities.[1] Even in the Soviet Union itself, numerous ethnic traditions were kept going (often under the guise of being merely regional folkways) despite official programs bent on the "effacement of national distinctions."[2] Only now, with the collapse of the Soviet state, are many of these long-suppressed traditions coming out into the open for the first time in decades.

The Social Spaces of Tradition

Before describing how traditions survive on their own, I want first to locate where they survive by mapping them socially. Just as a city has its particular locales of tradition, its old neighborhoods and historic districts, so too society as a whole has its special places where traditions can continue on with relatively little interference. Viewed spatially, traditions persist in four major sites: at the center of society, at the periphery, in the interstices, and underground.

Of the four sites, the center is the place where one would least expect to find naturally surviving traditions. For the most part, the center of society, like the center of the modern city, is occupied by the state, the market, and the culture industry; hence, it is where manipulated traditions predominate. Nevertheless, some autonomous traditions do survive without disguise and in full view. The religious traditions of the established churches are examples of nonmanipulated traditions that persist without obstruction at or near the center of society. The traditions kept intact by universities are another. Modern universities are certainly centrist institutions, yet they open up spaces which permit various literary, philosophical, and scientific traditions to exist and even to thrive with only a minimal amount of resistance. Similarly, mainstream political organizations preserve their own traditions, as do music conservatories, seminaries, cultural associations, and the like. In each of these examples, traditions can be said to survive at the center, but without being instrumentalized or commodified by the state or market.

When a tradition persists at the center of society, it may gain influence and visibility, but it also runs the risk of compromising itself. It is very difficult for a tradition to be sustained so close to power and money and not fall under their sway. Even if a centrist tradition remains autonomous, it can still lose much of its original character if its sharper edges are pared down, or if some of its untoward aspects are eliminated in order to make the tradition more acceptable. It is not unusual for supporters of centrist traditions to become overly defensive about what they are trying to uphold. As a result they often try too hard to demonstrate how salutary their traditions are for society as a whole. Furthermore, if a tradition is going to survive at the center it must become institutionalized so that it has the clout to protect itself against threats of cooptation. Today, mainline religious traditions need churches, political traditions need parties, and labor traditions need unions in order to safeguard their respective traditions in the public arena. There is little hope that any tradition can survive "naively" at the center of modern life simply on the basis of its own momentum, and without the added ballast of institutional support.

A second place where traditions have been able to survive on their own is at the margins of social life. It is here, in the corners and along the edges of society, that minority and subcultural traditions can find the space to maintain themselves, usually just barely out of view of the mainstream. Since the margins still remain public or semipublic locations, it is not as if such peripheral traditions have to hide in order to survive. It is simply that, for the sake of self-preservation, they must not call too much attention to themselves, but instead try to be as unobtrusive as possible. Typical marginal sites for subcultural traditions are ethnic communities, bohemian quarters of cities, or rural areas which have not been colonized by the center. Places such as these become protected environments where a variety of minority and parochial traditions not only survive but flourish. Even so, they survive at a price, for, by occupying the edge rather than the center, they are forced to reduce their claims and narrow their message to suit a smaller, more localized clientele. Many ethnic traditions have been circumscribed in this fashion, as have sectarian religious traditions. Political traditions which are unable to get a proper hearing at the center are also sometimes able to continue intact along the perimeters of social life. The so-called republican tradition, for instance, has managed to survive into our own time in fringe organizations or grass-roots associations, even though some of its basic tenets make it uncongenial to the political mainstream.[3] As a rule, the modern state, though it may prefer centrist traditions because they are easy to monitor, has been inclined to tolerate marginal traditions so long as they do not become threatening to the state itself. However, when marginal cultural or ethnic traditions become politicized in a radical or separatist direction—as has happened with the Basques and Catalans in Spain, the Croats and Slovenes in Yugoslavia, and the Irish in Britain—then the state generally becomes intolerant of such traditions and begins seeking ways to contain or suppress them.

A third place where autonomous traditions have survived is in the cracks and interstices of social existence. Here one finds a small range of cultural traditions and micropractices which have neither sought refuge at the margins nor become institutionalized at the center, but which have secured a foothold in the free spaces *within* modern society. In small nooks and crannies inside the social whole, these traditions and practices are able to continue on to the extent that they avoid the prying eyes of the state, the market, and the media. It is because they persist beyond the purview of established power that they do not normally have to protect themselves by becoming formally institutionalized, but rather can be passed down from one generation to another by word of mouth. Included in this third site of tradition is the entire private sphere of life, particularly the sphere of the family. Though the modern family is presently being assaulted and undermined by outside forces, it remains a place where private traditions can continue on relatively unimpeded. Usually these family traditions are inconsequential as far as the state or market is concerned, since they are centered around specific family memories, rituals, and ceremonies which—because they possess meaning only for the family members or relatives involved—do not lend themselves to outside appropriation. Nevertheless, as microscopic and seemingly unimportant as such traditions may be, they do occupy small pockets of space. When considered within the context of family life, they represent fully legitimate traditions.

A fourth and last site of unmanipulated traditions is underground. Today, at least some traditions exist not at the center, nor in the cracks, nor at the edges of social life, but below the surface. The most notable examples of subterranean traditions are those preserved by extremist religious sects, secret societies, and revolutionary political movements. When a religious group or a political faction transports a tradition underground, it is usually in order to find a hidden place for it to develop on its own. The semipublic spaces at the periphery and the unprotected spaces in the private sphere are generally judged unsafe, since both, being relatively undefended, are always susceptible to penetration by the center, even if such penetration is not generally the rule. To the adherents of subterranean traditions, the center always appears to be the enemy. Hence they seek a place for their tradition as far away from the center as possible, which often turns out to be underground and out of sight.

The history of the West offers numerous examples of dissenting religious traditions relocating underground mainly for their own protection. The early Christians retreated to the catacombs to avoid Roman persecutions. Medieval heretical groups such as the Brethren of the Free Spirit hid from the watchful eyes of the church and state for generations in order to maintain their beliefs in secret.[4] And surviving for centuries below the surface of the Judaism of the diaspora were a variety of clandestine mystical and eschatological traditions which somehow persisted despite the censure of rabbis and theologians.[5] In the twentieth century, both Christian and non-Christian millennarian sects have managed to preserve extremist religious traditions, but only by going underground and becoming as invisible as possible. Usually the choice of going underground is thought to be only a temporary measure. Most religious sects expect to reemerge into the light of day, strike down their enemies (or find that God has done so for them), and then make their traditions dominant. What is especially interesting about subterranean religious sects is that while they are underground they often do not temper their universalistic claims, but raise them to a higher level. Their seclusion weakens their capacity for reality testing, which in turn makes them still more militant and uncompromising. At the same time, the very hostility that underground religious traditions show toward a profane status quo proves to the established authorities that such traditions must be subversive in some way or other. Having reached this conclusion, the authorities often try that much harder to quash them, which naturally only confirms the sectarian conviction that the center must be evil if it so vigorously opposes what is godly.

There are also political traditions that move underground for protection. Some of these traditions are as uncompromising as the most extreme religious sects, but others, like the tradition of "council democracy," are relatively more moderate. As a radical offshoot of the republican tradition, council democracy has not been able to survive, as its progenitor has, at the periphery of society, but has had to live below the surface of normal politics for the 200 or so years of its existence. The term "council democracy" refers to a political tradition that calls for the direct participation of people in political decision making through the establishment of self-governing bodies that are immediately accessible to everyone, not mere bailiwicks of elected officials who claim to speak for the people-at-large. The term therefore designates a kind of democracy that is nonrepresentational, nonhierarchical, and decentralized—a kind dedicated to the practice of free, communal self-management. This tradition has lived a subterranean existence since the eighteenth century, mainly because it has been incompatible with dominant conceptions of what political power is and how it should be exercised. But from time to time the tradition of council democracy has resurfaced—apparently spontaneously—in revolutionary situations. It flared up in the Parisian municipal councils of 1793–94. It appeared again in the popular bodies of the Paris Commune in 1871, in the Petrograd Soviets of 1905 and 1917, and in the German *Räte* of 1918–19. It reemerged in the collectives of the Spanish Civil War and in the Hungarian Revolutionary Councils of 1956. And it surfaced during the May-June events in 1968 and in the Polish Solidarity Movement of 1980–81.

How does one explain the discontinuous history of a tradition like council democracy? At critical moments it seems to appear unexpectedly, be defeated, and then vanish for a generation or so; then it suddenly emerges again, apparently without any institutional support or sustenance, in some other time or place. The usual explanation is that it bursts forth spontaneously, as an expression of some intrinsic human urge toward self-determination. But a less essentialist explanation is possible. It may be that the ideas and practices associated with council democracy are carried forward by underground traditions which are not discernible to the naked eye, or at least not to the eye that scans only the surfaces of social or political life. In the case of council democracy, what

Hannah Arendt has called its striking and "entirely unexpected" reappearance from time to time may not really be so mysterious after all.[6] It might simply be due to the persistence of invisible (or at any rate, unobserved) lines of continuity concealed below the deceptively smooth surfaces of modern life.

The Cunning of Tradition

When a tradition survives without being artificially propped up, it is generally because it has been kept alive against all odds by the tenacity of its bearers and adherents. By surviving, however, the tradition finds itself subsisting in a context that is by no means conducive to it: a context dominated by a state, market, and culture industry whose basic collective interests are antitraditional. It is no wonder, then, that the supporters of such a tradition are likely to view the prospects of its continued existence with alarm. Under the circumstances it is natural for the defenders of the tradition to want to protect it by resettling it as far as possible from the centers of political and economic power. As I have said, this often means transporting it to the periphery of society, hiding it in the crevices of everyday life, removing it to the private sphere, or concealing it underground.

Every one of these modes of protection requires a certain amount of ingenuity. In each case a set of tactics has to be devised which will help preserve the tradition within an essentially hostile environment. By the term "tactics" I mean those methods of coping which must be improvised by a tradition's adherents in order to keep their particular tradition intact within a situation in which they do not control the "rules of the game." Wherever unequal forces are at play, in the world of animals no less than among human beings, the weaker party always resorts to tactics in its effort to confront the danger posed by the stronger party. And whenever tactics are utilized, one can find an assortment of ruses and ploys specifically designed by the powerless for their own preservation. Tactics are thus modes of adaptation based on cunning and connivance, dissemblance and subterfuge. They are the principal means by which the weak can slip by or around the strong and yet remain secure and unharmed. The stronger power, on the other hand, tends to operate in a completely different fashion: by means of a "strategy" rather than a set of tactics.[7] A strategy, which is based on force and coercion, makes sense for those who occupy the center within a field of power relations, since they can get what they want by means of intimidation. Thus, states and armies use strategies, not tactics, when they are formidable enough to function in terms of balances of power, zero-sum calculations, and the forced occupation of space by invasion or conquest. Where tactics are defensive, strategies are offensive; where tactics rely on a careful marshalling of resources, strategies can afford to be prodigal; and where tactics operate covertly, by means of deception and camouflage, strategies operate overtly, by means of an aggressive calculus of force-relations.[8]

If one looks at the nonmanipulated traditions still extant today, it is obvious that they have survived mainly by resorting to a wide variety of tactics: the tactic of *evasion* perfects the art of dodging, skirting, and circumventing; the tactic of *disguise* allows a tradition to stay at or near the center by masking or misrepresenting itself; with the tactic of *inversion,* a tradition withdraws or turns in upon itself at a moment of danger; in the tactic of *playing dead,* a tradition feigns inertness in order to appear harmless enough to be left alone; there is the tactic whereby a tradition *changes its content* to preserve its form, and a tactic whereby it *changes its form* to preserve its content;[9] and there is the tactic of *retreating,* at critical times, from a tradition of practice into a tradition of belief. This last tactic (which effectively encompasses many of the others as well) is employed on those occasions when it is too dangerous to act publicly on one's convictions. At such times necessity demands that a tradition of behavior transform itself into a tradition of thought or belief in order to survive in adverse conditions. Sometimes this transformation requires that a tradition of practice become a textual tradition. When a tradition becomes textual it is carried forward not by overt actions but by sacred books or hermetic writings, many of them made purposely incomprehensible or indecipherable to outsiders. Sometimes even textual traditions can be too dangerous if the established authorities prohibit them. When this happens, another tactic is possible: textual traditions can step back even further and become oral traditions. Here the tradition is passed on from one generation to the next solely by word of mouth with no material evidence, as far as the authorities are concerned, that the tradition is still alive.[10]

It is important to take note of the various tactics of tradition because we can learn something valuable simply from the manner by which they have managed to survive. We can learn how to maneuver in disadvantageous situations, how to bend without breaking, and how to operate by indirection, mastering the logic of the detour over the straight line. All of these skills may be important in a world that is in many ways becoming politically overadministered and economically overmanipulated. Today the balance of forces between the state or market, on the one hand, and the individual on the other, appears to be more unequal than it has ever been. Hence, there will probably be a greater need for people to devise ways to cope with situations which they have not helped shape, and which often militate against their own best interests. (Perhaps it will even become necessary, as Michel de Certeau has suggested, to begin forging new notions of what heroism is: notions that define the heroic as, among other things, the ability to survive against the current in a stream one does not and cannot control.)[11] In any event, by carefully observing the tactics of tradition, valuable lessons can be learned regarding what might be called practical resistance—lessons in how to be oppositional in such a way as to challenge the dominant tendencies of the present without being destroyed by them.

The tactics I have just described can be grasped by carefully examining the means and methods by which traditions survive in uncongenial settings. If one went no further than this, one would have creatively engaged enduring traditions—but only intellectually. To engage a tradition intellectually is certainly a worthwhile undertaking, but because the traditions I have been discussing in this chapter still persist, another option is possible: the option of engaging them directly and experientially. Only living traditions actually give a person the opportunity to enter into them, participate in them, and even advance or deepen them through his or her own activity. Before one actively "enters into" a tradition, however, some judgments should be made. First, it should be determined whether the tradition at issue is substantive. Some traditions, even those that have survived "naturally," are more symbolic than substantive if it is mainly their outward style and not their material content that has been preserved. In the United States, for instance, a number of ethnic traditions have become associated with particular tastes in food, clothing, and music, or with once-a-year ethnic holidays, but these are only the most superficial aspects of any tradition and should not be mistaken for the tradition *tout court*. To participate in a substantive as opposed to a symbolic tradition would probably require altering one's life, and not just one's "lifestyle." It would mean incorporating certain traditional habits of mind or patterns of behavior into one's daily existence instead of merely attaching oneself to the emblems or accoutrements of a tradition. This is not to say that there is anything inherently wrong with symbolic traditions, or that they have no place in modern life; it is only to point out that they are different than substantive traditions and should not be confused with them.[12]

A second judgment that needs to be made concerns the overall "value" of a tradition. Despite their tactical ingenuity in surviving, some traditions may not deserve active support. Today one can point to a number of enduring traditions that perpetuate bigotry and intolerance. If an individual were to insinuate himself into such traditions he would become, by virtually any standard of measurement, shallower and more narrow-minded. On the other hand, there are also traditions that appear to broaden the individuals who embrace them, particularly if such traditions provide qualities of thought or experience unavailable in the nontraditional mainstream. For example, today there are traditions that carry forward nearly forgotten spiritual legacies, and others that preserve irreplaceable elements of noncontemporaneity, and for these reasons both would seem worth upholding. Nevertheless, the matter of how to evaluate a tradition is a difficult one. In the last analysis, each individual may have to develop his or her own criteria of judgment based on questions such as: Does the tradition contain an element of truth which would be irretrievably lost if the tradition did not survive? Is it creatively enabling, making possible a more enriched presence in the world? Is it a source of real heterogeneity and diversity which should not be allowed to disappear? Does the tradition help advance critical consciousness? Does it promote individual autonomy and responsibility, or strengthen moral self-awareness?

These are, of course, only suggestions. But if one takes the opportunity not only to learn from the tactics of tradition but to participate actively in those traditions that seem worth affirming, one then moves beyond an intellectual and into a praxical relationship to tradition. To be sure, there is something problematic about the notion of *choosing* to become involved in a tradition. By intentionally joining a tradition instead of merely being born into one, the modern individual finds himself very far removed from those periods in the past when being in a tradition was simply taken for granted. In earlier times, to be enveloped by traditional ways of life was part of normal, everyday experience. Today, however, there are very few traditions that people in the West can be in naturally and unreflectively. We have been permanently driven out of such a condition of naiveté by the forces of modernity. There is no way to reverse what has happened historically, nor would it even be desirable to go back to the way things were. Yet ironically there is a gain in this loss, for to choose to adhere to a tradition, and to remain consciously and willfully committed to it, may represent something qualitatively higher than merely being in a tradition by accident.

9 Conclusion

Everyone living in today's Western world lives in modernity. Even those who speak of postmodernity have not made a convincing case that the West has entered into a distinctly new era. Postmodernity simply extends and reworks, but does not transcend, the main elements of modernity.[1]

To say that modernity is now our enveloping reality, however, does not mean that we have determined how to assess it. While some observers assume a predominantly hostile attitude toward modernity, others regard it as fundamentally emancipatory. In the first camp, as we have seen, modernity has come to mean the fragmentation of the lifeworld, the atomization of experience, and the desacralization of values. Each of these developments is taken to be a loss, and the main underlying cause that produced them is said to be the decline of tradition in modern life. But, as tradition disappears, so does the social cement that has historically bound people together in integrated communities. Several institutions, cognizant of this problem, have tried to fill the void which they themselves helped create. Hence, the state has come forward with administrative rationality, the market with consumerism, and the electronic media with mass culture. But critics of modernity believe that all of these substitutes have failed to replace the glue of tradition. As proof of this contention, they point to the widespread erosion of community, the dissolution of authority, the growth in crime and violence, and the increasing normlessness of modern social life. According to many of these critics, the solution to present-day disintegration must lie in a return to tradition—a return that tries to renew the legacies of the past, or, where that is impossible, to at least preserve and respectfully cherish the few links to the past that yet remain.

131

In direct opposition to this perspective, another camp regards modernity not as destructive but as liberatory. For these commentators, modernity is synonymous with an expansion of the realm of freedom, more individual autonomy, new possibilities for self-expression, and general material betterment. They agree that tradition has declined, but this development is celebrated rather than lamented, since this second camp regards tradition as little more than the cumulative weight of inherited norms, prescriptions, and injunctions that only serve to deaden the human spirit. The demise of tradition is therefore viewed as a positive development, in that people will now be freer to embrace immediacy, exult in the variety of the present, and, if they choose, simply "play with the pieces" left over from the traditional past.[2]

In my opinion, neither of these positions is quite on the mark. The first is right to be critical of the present, but wrong to think that the past offers viable alternatives. The second is right to accept modernity, but wrong to take such an approbative attitude toward it. The stance of accepting the present while at the same time remaining critical of it— which is the one I am suggesting here—naturally leads one to an immanent critique of modernity.

An immanent critique starts out with the givens of modern life but sees them as inherently deficient, since modernity is so much less than what it could or should be. Locked within the givens are, it is assumed, potentialities not yet realized, in light of which the present cannot help but seem flawed, defective, and incomplete. Nonetheless, instead of rejecting the world-as-it-is, an immanent critique chooses to work with and through its very inadequacies. One way of doing this is by focusing on the contradictions between a society's ideals and its stark realities. By driving factual reality toward its own highest possibilities, an immanent critique seeks to turn mere potentiality into actuality. The key to its method is to work within a given framework in such a manner as to push its inherent tensions and contradictions toward higher resolutions. The obverse of an immanent critique is the so-called total critique of society, which sees *no* unrealized possibilities that can be salvaged, and which therefore rejects the present in its entirety and seeks to replace it with something completely different. To some extent, one finds this kind of total critique in Heidegger, who treated the technocratic world of late capitalism as morally corrupt and tragically "fallen." One can find it as well in the pre-Marxist Lukács, who described the same capitalist world as lost in "soulless immediacy" and "utter degradation." Both thinkers doubted that what they considered the sickness of modernity could be remedied with larger doses of modernity. Instead, health could only be restored through a transformation, or "redemption," of the entire body politic. This notion led each to search for an agent of redemption that would somehow save modernity from itself. Lukács eventually found this agent in the proletariat, and Heidegger found it, briefly, in the National Socialist movement.[3]

In my view, the immanent critique of society—and not the total critique—represents the best approach we currently have for engaging modernity on its own terms. But in practice, it has not always produced the gains it seems to promise in theory. For instance, even when an immanent critique exposes the aporias and contradictions in social life, nothing usually changes. The truth of the critique may be acknowledged, but nothing is done about it. One reason for the apparent ineffectiveness of an immanent critique today may lie in what one critic has termed "the entrenched cynicism of bourgeois society *vis-à-vis* its own universalistic normative foundations."[4] If ideals are no longer taken seriously, then to point out how far we are from actualizing them would carry no critical weight. Real contradictions would be treated as mere discrepancies to be patched up or papered over, and in time the way-things-are would come to be viewed as more or less the way-things-should-be. If an outlook such as this became dominant, as many think it already is, there would be little reason to *do* anything, and the whole forward thrust of immanent critique would be put in jeopardy.

Perhaps it was with just this thought in mind that the historian Marshall Berman has made an interesting suggestion. Believing that we are in many respects stuck in a sterile present, Berman has proposed that we imaginatively return to an earlier, more creative moment *within* modernity. That "moment," in his opinion, should be the early to mid-nineteenth century, a period of an especially intense liveliness and vitality which can still be tapped in our own time. There is thus a need to return to the "roots" of modernity in order to recover the freshness, depth, and resonance that seem to be missing in the late twentieth century. If this original energy could be drawn on once again, the project of modernity could be put back on track. Even the flagging immanent critique, which has always been an essential part of modernity, could be revitalized and restored to some of its initial power. As Berman expressed it in *All That Is Solid Melts into Air:* "It may turn out, then, that going back can be a way to go forward: that remembering the modernisms of the nineteenth century can give us the vision and courage to create the modernisms of the twenty-first. This act of remembering can help us bring modernism back to its roots, so that it can nourish and renew itself. . . . To appropriate the modernities of yesterday can be at once a critique of the modernities of today and an act of faith in the modernities . . . of tomorrow, and the day after tomorrow."[5]

This position is appealing, and I am in full agreement with Berman regarding the importance of renewing modernity from its origins, while at the same time not abandoning the perspective of immanent critique. Still, the one problem with Berman's suggestion is that all of his answers to the malaise of modernity lie entirely within the framework of modernity. Because he makes no reference to the otherness that exists *beyond* the modern context, he does not go far enough in seeking leverage against the shortcomings of modernity. But, as I have argued throughout this book, we do have continuing access to various forms of noncontemporaneous otherness; they exist in surviving fragments of lapsed traditions, in traces hidden away in refunctioned traditions, and even in some enduring (but silenced or marginalized) traditions that can yet be experienced firsthand.

It is my view that we should take a careful look at these residual traditions, or parts of traditions, but always with the understanding that they can be helpful in expanding and augmenting, not replacing, the project of immanent critique. What is valuable about the neglected or discarded material from the past is that it is noncompliant, nonidentical, and even oppositional to the present. Because at least some traditions possess these refractory qualities, they do not have to be thought of as the exclusive property of conservatives. Instead, they can be seen as containing a radical as well as a conservative dimension, particularly to the extent that they are able to offer a perspective on modernity from the point of view of what modernity has excluded.

This is the kind of perspective that I believe we need today. Too often in the modern period, those traditions that have survived have been treated as outmoded vestiges from the past, the debris of history. Those traditions that have not survived have usually been considered useless by modern standards, and therefore hardly worth salvaging. It is true, there is much from the traditional past that does not deserve rescue, but there is also much that is of great value. Simply because a tradition was defeated does not speak against it, for to be vanquished indicates no lack of worth, only that the adversary was stronger. Likewise, just because

134

other traditions have been forced to the periphery of social life—or worse, commodified and instrumentalized—does not mean they are without value. On the contrary, what I think is required now is a recuperation of exactly those traditions that have been dismissed, censured, occluded, marginalized, surpassed, or suppressed. We need to reconsider what might be called the refuse of the dialectic, not in order to increase social cohesion or promote a *restitutio in integrum*, but in order to acquire a vantage point on modernity based on what modernity has banished or repressed.

The reappropriation of tradition is, in itself, no alternative to an immanent critique of modernity. It is only a means to broaden and deepen the methods of immanent critique by tapping into a wealth of material that normally lies outside its range. As I have tried to show, this material includes the nonsynchronous elements of discontinued traditions, as well as the surplus or excess meanings still present in continuing ones. Both kinds of difference are valuable because they provoke contradictions, challenge modern technologies of power and control, and provide access to alternate ways of being and thinking which we cannot afford to be without. Thus, in contrast to anything our forebears could have said, the critical importance of tradition may now lie in its apparent obsolescence. If this is so, then the words Novalis penned two centuries ago (cited in the epigraph) concerning the need to look back in order to go forward may still be true for our own time, but perhaps in a completely different sense than Novalis intended.

Notes

Introduction

1. Edmund Burke, *Reflections on the Revolution in France,* ed. William B. Todd (New York: Rinehart & Company, 1959), p. 117.

2. Adolf Erman, *Die Literatur der Aegypter* (Leipzig: J. C. Hinrichs, 1923), pp. 130ff.

3. Martin Heidegger, *Der Spiegel* interview (1976), cited in *Heidegger: The Man and the Thinker,* ed. James Sheehan (Chicago: Precedent, 1981), p. 57.

4. Edward Shils, *Tradition* (London: Faber and Faber, 1981), pp. 21–23, 303–10.

5. See Susan Buck-Morss, "Semiotic Boundaries and the Politics of Meaning: Modernity on Tour—A Village in Transition," in *New Ways of Knowing: The Sciences, Society, and Reconstructive Knowledge,* ed. Marcus G. Raskin and Herbert J. Bernstein (Towata: Rowman & Littlefield, 1987), p. 222.

1. The Meaning of Tradition

1. J.G.A. Pocock, *Politics, Language, and Time: Essays on Political Thought and History* (New York: Atheneum, 1971), p. 237.

2. See Max Radin, "Tradition," *Encyclopaedia of the Social Sciences,* vol. 15, ed. Edwin Seligman and Alvin Johnson (New York: Macmillan, 1937), p. 63.

3. For a more detailed discussion of the elements that constitute a tradition, see Edward Shils, *Tradition* (London: Faber and Faber, 1981), pp. 1–33; and Josef Pieper, *Überlieferung* (Munich: Kösel Verlag, 1970), pp. 21–41.

4. On the survival of Cathari and Waldensian traditions, see Steven Runciman, *The Medieval Manichee: A Study of the Christian Dualist Heresy* (New York: Viking, 1961); and Pierre Belperron, *La Croisade contre Les Albigeois* (Paris: Librairie Plon, 1948).

5. See the several essays on Jewish tradition in *Jewish Culture and Identity in the Soviet Union,* ed. Yaacov Ro'i and Avi Beker (New York: New York University Press, 1991).

6. Radin, "Tradition," p. 62.

7. Max Weber, *Economy and Society,* vol. 1, ed. Günther Roth and Claus Wit-

tich, trans. Ephraim Fischoff (Berkeley: University of California Press, 1978), p. 319.

8. See Michel de Certeau, *The Practices of Everyday Life*, trans. Steven F. Rendall (Berkeley: University of California Press, 1984), pp. 64–68.

9. Traditions, no less than the "truths" Nietzsche talked about, are like old coins: in the course of being handed down they sometimes lose their engraved pictures, and then eventually their original value. When this happens, they become (in Nietzsche's terms) "worn out," shorn of their "sensuous power." After a while, traditions, like truths, come to "matter only as metal, no longer as coins." See Friedrich Nietzsche, "On Truth and Lie in an Extra-Moral Sense," in *The Portable Nietzsche*, trans. Walter Kaufmann (New York: Viking, 1962), p. 47.

10. Alterations of the tradition might seem to purists of the transmitting generation like a willful falsification of what is handed down. But blatant, intentional falsification is not generally the rule. What appears to be a misappropriation may actually be (from the receiving generation's perspective) an appropriation made in good faith. All traditions have to be modified somewhat in the process of being acquired and put into practice.

11. Alisdair MacIntyre, *Whose Justice? Whose Rationality?* (Notre Dame: University of Notre Dame Press, 1988), p. 326.

12. See Hans-Georg Gadamer, *Truth and Method*, trans. Garrett Barden and John Cumming (New York: Crossroad, 1965), pp. 250, 252–53.

13. On the effects of writing on tradition, see Jack Goody, *Domestication of the Savage Mind* (Cambridge: Cambridge University Press, 1977), esp. chaps. 2 and 3; and Jack Goody, *The Logic of Writing and the Organization of Society* (Cambridge: Cambridge University Press, 1986).

14. See the comments by Brian Stock in *Listening for the Text: On the Uses of the Past* (Baltimore: Johns Hopkins University Press, 1990), pp. 19–23; and M. T. Clanchy, *From Memory to Written Record: England, 1066–1307* (Cambridge: Harvard University Press, 1979).

15. Stock, *Listening*, pp. 144–46. See also Brian Stock, *Implications of Literacy: Written Language and Models of Interpretation in the Eleventh and Twelfth Centuries* (Princeton: Princeton University Press, 1983), pp. 30–87; Yves Congar, *The Meaning of Tradition*, trans. A. N. Woodrow (New York: Hawthorn Books, 1964), pp. 14–47, 79–119; Gershom Scholem's two essays, "The Crisis of Tradition in Jewish Messianism" and "Martin Buber's Interpretation of Hasidism," in *The Messianic Idea in Judaism* (New York: Schocken, 1971), pp. 49–77, 227–50; and Michel Vovelle, "Popular Religion," *Ideologies and Mentalities*, trans. Eamon O'Flaherty (Chicago: University of Chicago Press, 1990), pp. 81–113.

16. Shils, *Tradition*, pp. 44–46; Hans Freyer, *Theorie des gegenwärtigen Zeitalters* (Stuttgart: Deutsche Verlags-Anstalt, 1956), pp. 93–99, 176–90.

2. Tradition under Stress

1. On the importance of origins in archaic societies, see especially Mircea Eliade, *Myth and Reality*, trans. Willard R. Trask (New York: Harper and Row, 1963), pp. 21–53.

2. The term "little traditions" is Robert Redfield's. See his *Peasant Society and Culture* (Chicago: University of Chicago Press, 1960), pp. 41–45.

3. To be sure, innovative elements did emerge in the Renaissance and Reformation, but paradoxically many of these innovations came about not through the discovery of something entirely new, but by reviving older traditions which seemed neglected or forgotten. The Renaissance, for example, rejected many of the regnant medieval cultural and intellectual traditions in order to restore others associated with the classical heritage which had allegedly been lost sight of during what Petrarch called the "dark centuries" of the Middle Ages. Likewise, the Reformation was not hostile to tradition per se, but only to Catholic doctrinal traditions which had accumulated over the centuries, and which seemed to obscure the more valuable traditions of the early Church. What the reformers wanted above all was a *nostos*—a return—to the original, "authentic" traditions of the Apostolic Age and immediately after, i.e., *before* they were corrupted by Catholic exegesis. In both cases—the Renaissance and Reformation—there was not a forward-looking attitude so much as there was an interest in some kind of *restitutio in integrum*, which in its essential elements was not inherently anti-traditional. On the Renaissance, see Werner Beierwaltes, "Subjektivität, Schöpfertum, Freiheit: Die Philosophie der Renaissance zwischen Tradition und neuzeitlichem Bewusstsein," in *Der Übergang zur Neuzeit und die Wirkung von Traditionen*, papers presented to the Joachim Jungius-Gesellschaft (Göttingen: Vandenhoeck and Ruprecht, 1978), pp. 15–31. On the Reformation, see Jaroslav Pelikan, *Obedient Rebels: Catholic Substance and Protestant Principle in Luther's Reformation* (New York: Harper and Row, 1964), pp. 27–53.

4. See Hans Blumenberg, *The Legitimacy of the Modern Age*, trans. Robert M. Wallace (Cambridge: MIT Press, 1983), pp. 107, 381. This almost unrestrained optimism concerning man's creative potential is evident in all Bacon's works, but perhaps especially in his preface to *The Great Instauration* (1620), the *Novum Organum* (1620), and *The Advancement of Learning* (1605).

5. As an author, Bacon himself intentionally wrote in such a way as to utilize traditional metaphors, allusions, and figurative associations to express novel ideas. The best discussion of this, and of Bacon's relation to tradition in general, can be found in Charles Whitney, *Francis Bacon and Modernity* (New Haven: Yale University Press, 1986), esp. chaps. 3 and 4.

6. Ibid., pp. 56–60, 96–98, 144, 151–52.

7. René Descartes, *Discourse on Method*, trans. Laurence J. Lafleur (Indianapolis: Bobbs-Merrill, 1977), p. 7.

8. Ibid., p. 9 (my italics).

9. The one exception: only if the world comes to an end, and all the vestiges of the first beginning lie in ruins, can a second beginning occur. See Eliade, *Myth and Reality*, pp. 51–52.

10. See Hannah Arendt, *On Revolution* (New York: Viking, 1968), pp. 205–15.

11. Niccolo Machiavelli, cited in Bruce Jennings, "Tradition and the Politics of Remembering," *Georgia Review* 36, no. 1 (Spring 1982): 170. For Machiavelli, the return to the beginnings was the key to religious as well as political renewal.

Thus in his *Discourses* he pointed out that, by virtue of their voluntary poverty, St. Francis and St. Dominic had returned to "first principles"—that is, to the "example of Christ's life which they revived . . . when it had almost been extinguished." See *The Discourses of Niccolo Machiavelli*, trans. and annot. Leslie J. Walker (London: Routledge and Kegan Paul, 1950), bk. 3, sec. 2.

12. See Edward Said, *Beginnings: Intention and Method* (New York: Basic Books, 1975), pp. 13, 34, 39, 47.

13. See, for example, Francis Bacon, *Novum Organon,* in *The Works of Francis Bacon,* vol. 4, ed. James Spedding, R. L. Ellis, and D. D. Heath (London: Longmans and Co., 1883), p. 52; and René Descartes, *Meditations,* trans. Laurence J. Lafleur (Indianapolis: Bobbs-Merrill, 1977), p. 75.

14. See Thomas Hobbes, *Leviathan* (New York: E. P. Dutton, 1950), pp. 142–44.

15. Samuel Pufendorf, *Of the Law of Nature and Nations,* vol. 7, 2d ed., trans. Basil Kennett (Oxford: A. and J. Churchil, 1710), chap. 2, sec. 6; see also Horst Denzer, *Moralphilosophie und Naturrecht bei Samuel Pufendorf* (Munich: Verlag C. H. Beck, 1972), pp. 100–06.

16. The language is that of Francis Bacon speaking particularly about the traditional forms of human knowledge which he opposed. See Francis Bacon, *The Great Instauration,* in *Works,* vol. 4, pp. 7–8; also Whitney, *Francis Bacon,* p. 91.

17. Max Weber, *The Protestant Ethic and the Spirit of Capitalism,* trans. Talcott Parsons (New York: Scribners, 1958); Werner Sombart, *Der Bourgeois: Zur Geistesgeschichte des modernen Wirtschaftsmenschen* (Munich: Duncker and Humblot, 1913).

18. Weber, *The Protestant Ethic,* pp. 18, 77. This argument is made, for example, in Luciano Pellicani, "Weber and the Myth of Calvinism," *Telos* 75 (Summer 1988): 57–85. For an opposing point of view, see Guy Oakes, "Farewell to the Protestant Ethic?" *Telos* 78 (Winter 1988–89): 81–94.

19. See Albert O. Hirschman, *The Passions and the Interests: Political Arguments for Capitalism before Its Triumph* (Princeton: Princeton University Press, 1977).

20. See, for instance, Régine Pernoud, *Histoire de la bourgeoisie en France,* vol. 1 (Paris: Éditions du Seuil, 1960), pp. 373–94, 427–42; and Charles and Katherine George, "Protestantism and Capitalism in Pre-Revolutionary England," in *The Protestant Ethic and Modernization,* ed. S. N. Eisenstadt (New York: Basic Books, 1968), pp. 155–76.

21. Gianfranco Poggi, *The Development of the Modern State* (Stanford: Stanford University Press, 1978). For a somewhat different view, see Perry Anderson, *Lineages of the Absolutist State* (London: New Left Books, 1974).

22. Cornelia Navari, "The Origins of the Nation-State," in *The Nation-State: The Formation of Modern Politics,* ed. Leonard Tivey (New York: St. Martin's Press, 1981), pp. 32–33.

23. There is much evidence to indicate the cooptive power of French absolutism as I have described it here, but one must be careful not to exaggerate its breadth and depth. Recent scholarship has warned that France under Louis XIV

was in many respects more deeply enmeshed in traditional feudal and corporate structures than was previously realized. Though in my view French absolutism was by its very nature antitraditional, it could also accommodate itself to tradition when that option was advantageous, i.e., it could work within traditional forms and even defend the very feudal-agrarian interests which in most other respects it opposed. See William Beik, *Absolutism and Society in Seventeenth-Century France* (Cambridge: Cambridge University Press, 1985), pp. 18–33, 329–39; David Parker, *The Making of French Absolutism* (New York: St. Martin's Press, 1983), pp. 81–91, 136–45; François Dumont, "French Kingship and Absolute Monarchy in the Seventeenth Century," in *Louis XIV and Absolutism*, ed. Ragnhild Hatton (Columbus: Ohio State University Press, 1976), pp. 55–84. But for another point of view, see Roland Mousnier, *Les Institutions de la France sous la monarchie absolue 1598–1789*, 2 vols. (Paris: Presses universitaires de France, 1974–80).

24. Mark Raeff, "The Well-Ordered Police State and the Development of Modernity in Seventeenth- and Eighteenth-Century Europe," *American Historical Review*, 80, no. 5 (December 1975): 1226.

25. Marc Raeff, *The Well-Ordered Police State* (New Haven: Yale University Press, 1983), p. 85. See also Hans Rosenberg, *Bureaucracy, Aristocracy, and Autocracy: The Prussian Experience, 1660–1815* (Boston: Beacon Press, 1966); and Gerhard Oestreich, *Geist und Gestalt des frühmodernen Staates* (Berlin: Duncker and Humblot, 1969).

26. See Otto von Gierke, *Natural Law and the Theory of Society, 1500–1800*, trans. Ernest Barker (Cambridge: Cambridge University Press, 1934), pp. 62–92, 162–80; and David Gross, "Temporality and the Modern State," *Theory and Society* 14 (1985): 53–82.

27. On traditional and rational authority, see Max Weber, *Economy and Society*, vol. 1, pp. 217–31; and Wolfgang Schluchter, *The Rise of Western Rationalism: Max Weber's Developmental Theory*, trans. Günther Roth (Berkeley: University of California Press, 1981), pp. 106–21.

28. John Locke, "Second Treatise on Government," in *Treatise of Civil Government and a Letter Concerning Toleration*, ed. Charles L. Sherman (New York: Appleton-Century-Crofts, 1965), p. 67.

29. Immanuel Kant, "What is Enlightenment?" in *The Enlightenment: A Comprehensive Anthology*, ed. Peter Gay (New York: Simon and Schuster, 1973), pp. 383–90.

30. For the Enlightenment view of aristocratic traditions, see the summary discussion in Robert Anchor, *The Enlightenment Tradition* (New York: Harper and Row, 1967), pp. 6–33. On the Enlightenment view of the peasantry, see Henry C. Payne, *The Philosophes and the People* (New Haven: Yale University Press, 1976), pp. 7–31.

31. The best treatment of the philosophe view of happiness is Robert Mauzi's *L'idée du bonheur dans la littérature et la pensée françaises au XVIIIᵉ siècle* (Paris: Librairie Armand Colin, 1960). On the importance of freedom for the Enlightenment, see the entry "Liberté" in the *Encyclopédie, ou dictionnaire raisonné, des sciences, des arts et des métiers*, vol. 19, ed. Denis Diderot (Geneva: Pellet, 1777),

pp. 979–96; and Bronislaw Baczko, "Die französische Aufklärung und die Philosophie des Konkreten," *Weltanschauung, Metaphysik, Entfremdung: Philosophische Versuche* (Frankfurt: Suhrkamp, 1969), pp. 80–94.

32. See the entries "Habitude" and "Philosophe" in the *Encyclopédie* cited above, vol. 16, pp. 887–89, and vol. 25, pp. 667–70, respectively.

33. On the process of *Landflucht* in Germany, see Hubert Kiesewetter, *Industrielle Revolution in Deutschland, 1815–1914* (Frankfurt: Suhrkamp, 1980), pp. 147–64. On England, see N. L. Tranter, *Population and Society, 1750–1940* (London and New York: Longman, 1985), pp. 37–43. The exodus from rural to urban areas was both less extensive and more complicated in France. See Eugen Weber, *Peasants into Frenchmen: The Modernization of Rural France, 1870–1914* (Stanford: Stanford University Press, 1976), pp. 278–91.

34. The best estimate of the total number of people who emigrated *from* Europe overseas—and therefore not counting those who migrated from one region to another, or from the country to the city, *within* Europe—is 55 million between 1820 and 1924 (or 50 million between the 1840s and 1914). Of this number probably 60 to 70 percent were peasants, small farmers, or rural day-laborers. See *International Migrations*, vol. 1, ed. Walter F. Willcox (New York, London, and Paris: Gordon and Breach, 1969), esp. pp. 81–86; and Frank Thistlethwaite, "Migrations from Europe Overseas in the Nineteenth and Twentieth Centuries," *Population Movements in Modern European History*, ed. Herbert Moller (New York: Macmillan, 1964), pp. 73–92.

35. The result of this tardiness for the new urban dwellers was either a snapping of religious traditions altogether, or an attraction to a variety of religious cults or "labor sects" outside the framework of the established churches. See Eric Hobsbawm, *Labouring Men: Studies in the History of Labour* (London: Weidenfeld and Nicolson, 1964), pp. 23–33.

36. On this see Niel J. Smelser, "The Modernization of Social Relations," in *Modernization: The Dynamics of Growth*, ed. Myron Weiner (New York: Basic Books, 1966), pp. 118–19. In America, for instance, it appears that it was older emigrant women (who never entered the work force) who did the most to preserve traditional values by keeping them alive within family settings. By contrast, most younger emigrants, male and female, abandoned Old-World traditions rather rapidly as a result of three kinds of pressures: the drive toward Americanization in the schools; the stress in the workplace to drop traditional orientations in the interest of personal advancement; and the enticements of an emerging consumer culture, which emphasized the importance of buying and owning things over loyalty to the antiquated values of the past. See Elizabeth Ewen, *Immigrant Women in the Land of Dollars* (New York: Monthly Review Press, 1985), pp. 76–91, 186–205.

37. On the *social* meaning of the lifeworld, see especially Alfred Schutz, *The Phenomenology of the Social World*, trans. George Walsh and Frederick Lehnert (Evanston: Northwestern University Press, 1987), pp. 139–214; Alfred Schutz and Thomas Luckmann, *The Structure of the Life-World*, trans. Richard Zaner and H. Tristram Engelhardt, Jr. (Evanston: Northwestern University Press, 1973), pp. 4–11, 59–61; and Jürgen Habermas, *The Theory of Communicative*

Action, vol. 2, trans. Thomas McCarthy (Boston: Beacon Press, 1987), pp. 113–52.

3. Shaking the Foundations

1. Jürgen Habermas, "The New Obscurity," *Philosophy and Social Criticism* 11, no. 2 (Winter 1986): 1.

2. The literature on modernity is extensive, but see especially Hans Blumenberg, *The Legitimacy of the Modern Age,* trans. Robert M. Wallace (Cambridge: MIT Press, 1983); Jürgen Habermas, *The Philosophical Discourse of Modernity,* trans. Frederick Lawrence (Cambridge: MIT Press, 1987); Jürgen Habermas, *The Theory of Communicative Action,* 2 vols., trans. Thomas McCarthy (Boston: Beacon Press, 1984, 1987); Reinhart Koselleck, *Futures Past: On the Semantics of Historical Time,* trans. Keith Tribe (Cambridge: MIT Press, 1985); David McClelland, *The Achieving Society* (New York: Irvington, 1976); and Anthony Giddens, *The Consequences of Modernity* (Stanford: Stanford University Press, 1990).

3. Ralph Waldo Emerson, *Nature* (Boston and New York: Houghton, Mifflin, and Co., 1883), p. 3. At almost the same time Tocqueville observed that among Americans, "the tie that unites one generation to another is being relaxed or broken [with the result that everyone] . . . readily loses all trace of the ideas of his forefathers or takes no care about them." According to Tocqueville, if tradition is remembered at all, it is only as a "means of information," or a marker to indicate how far one has moved from some fixed point in the past. Alexis de Tocqueville, *Democracy in America,* vol. 2, Henry Reeve text, ed. Phillips Bradley (New York: Knopf, 1946), pp. 3–4.

4. See R.W.B. Lewis, *The American Adam* (Chicago: University of Chicago Press, 1955), pp. 5, 9, 13–27.

5. Jeremy Bentham, *The Book of Fallacies* (1824), pp. 27, 77, 80; cited in Raymond Chapman, *The Sense of the Past in Victorian Literature* (New York: St. Martin's Press, 1986), p. 176.

6. The classical statement of this development is Georg Simmel's "The Metropolis and Mental Life," in *The Sociology of Georg Simmel,* trans. Kurt H. Wolff (Glencoe: The Free Press, 1964), pp. 409–24.

7. Habermas, *Theory of Communicative Action,* vol. 2, p. 116.

8. Ibid., pp. 302, 355.

9. George Kubler, *The Shape of Time* (New Haven: Yale University Press, 1979), pp. 77–79. Some excellent examples of how tradition can be weakened as a result of greater material abundance can be found in Eugen Weber, *Peasants into Frenchmen: The Modernization of Rural France* (Stanford: Stanford University Press, 1976), esp. pp. 377–98, 413–18, 471–96.

10. Jürgen Habermas, *Legitimation Crisis,* trans. Thomas McCarthy (Boston: Beacon Press, 1975), pp. 73, 75–82, 92–93.

11. Of course, institutional rationality was created in the first place by those "on top." It did not evolve on its own as part of some ineluctable universalizing tendency, though in retrospect this is sometimes the impression one gets. In-

stead, those significant groups which founded industrial enterprises or bureaucratic states were, at least at first, the true carriers of rationality, for it was they who actively encouraged more order, rigor, and dependability in modern life in order either to increase production or to guarantee compliance with the law. Once encompassing rational structures were in place, however, they obviously helped shape the behavior of others "down below" (employees, civil servants, industrial laborers) who had no choice but to be drawn into and shaped by them. See Wolfgang Mommsen, "Personal Conduct and Societal Change," in *Max Weber: Rationality and Modernity*, ed. Scott Lash and Sam Whimster (London: Allen and Unwin, 1987), pp. 35–51.

12. See Michel Foucault, *Discipline and Punish*, trans. Alan Sheridan (New York: Vintage, 1979); M. Christine Boyer, *Dreaming the Rational City* (Cambridge: MIT Press, 1983); and Christopher Dandeker, *Surveillance, Power and Modernity: Bureaucracy and Discipline from 1700 to the Present Day* (New York: St. Martin's Press, 1990).

13. See David Gross, "Temporality and the Modern State," *Theory and Society* 14 (1985): 53–82; and David Gross, "Space, Time and Modern Culture," *Telos* 50 (Winter 1981–82): 59–78.

14. Robert Michels was one of the first to analyze this process in some detail. See Robert Michels, *Political Parties: A Sociological Study of the Oligarchical Tendencies of Modern Democracy*, trans. Eden and Cedar Paul (1911; New York: Collier, 1962), esp. pp. 333–41.

15. On Rudorff's *Deutsche Heimatschutzbewegung*, see Richard Hamann and Jost Hermand, *Stilkunst um 1900*, vol. 4 of *Epochen deutscher Kultur von 1870 bis zur Gegenwart* (Frankfurt: Fischer Verlag, 1977), pp. 327–29. Some aspects of the institutionalization of right-wing ideologies are treated in Zeev Sternhell, *La droite révolutionnaire 1885–1914: les origines françaises du fascisme* (Paris: Éditions du Seuil, 1978); and George L. Mosse, *The Crisis of German Ideology* (New York: Grosset and Dunlap, 1964).

16. Weber, *Economy and Society*, vol. 1, p. 85.

17. Max Weber articulated this position most forcefully, but others at the time concurred. See Harry Liebersohn, *Fate and Utopia in German Sociology, 1870– 1923* (Cambridge: MIT Press, 1988); and David Gross, "Weber in Context: The Dilemmas of Modernity," *Telos* 78 (Winter 1988–89): 109–17.

The distinction between technical and substantive rationality was later picked up by Lukács, who identified substantive rationality with communism, and technical rationality with a decadent late capitalism. The same distinction continued on in the Frankfurt School, but with a different slant. Horkheimer, for example, argued for the need to "bring [more] reason into the world," and Marcuse equated the fullness of humanity with the fullness of rationality ("Reason represents the highest potentiality of man and existence"). But when the Critical Theorists spoke of reason in this way, they had only substantive rationality in mind. For them, a continuation of technical or instrumental rationality would only lead to what Adorno called a "totally administered society." (On this see Richard Wolin, "Critical Theory and the Dialectic of Rationalism," *New German Critique* 41, [Spring-Summer 1987]: 23–52.) Some of these notions have also found their way into the work of Habermas, though he seems to think that substantive rationality can never be achieved. To assume that the world could be transformed or made whole is, for him, a purely utopian fantasy. What *can* be achieved, however, is what Habermas calls discursive or communicative rationality (a rationality based on the intersubjective resolution of validity claims in formal argumentation); this type of reason appears to fall somewhere between instrumental and substantive rationality. For a discussion of communicative rationality, see especially Habermas's *Theory of Communicative Action* (cited above); and Seyla Benhabib, "Modernity and the Aporias of Critical Theory," *Telos* 49 (Fall 1981): 38–60.

18. See Sigmund Freud, *Group Psychology and the Analysis of the Ego*, trans. James Strachey (1921; New York: Bantam, 1965), pp. 3–18, 78–84.

19. The best brief account of this development, particularly within the American context, can be found in T. J. Jackson Lears, *No Place of Grace: Antimodernism and the Transformation of American Culture, 1880–1920* (New York: Pantheon, 1981), pp. 35–58, 218–25.

20. Werner Sombart, *Der Bourgeois: Zur Geistesgeschichte des modernen Wirtschaftsmenschen* (Munich: Duncker and Humblot, 1913), pp. 194–243.

21. Max Weber, cited in Arthur Mitzman, *The Iron Cage: An Historical Interpretation of Max Weber* (New Brunswick: Transaction Books, 1985), p. 217.

22. This is a commonplace now, but Georg Simmel noted it already in 1900 in his *Philosophie des Geldes*. See Georg Simmel, *The Philosophy of Money*, trans. Tom Bottomore and David Frisby (London: Routledge and Kegan Paul, 1978), p. 484; and David Frisby, "Georg Simmel: First Sociologist of Modernity," *Theory, Culture and Society* 2, no. 3 (1985); 49–67.

23. See O. F. Bollnow, *Die Lebensphilosophie* (Berlin: Springer-Verlag, 1958); Max Nordau, *Die conventionellen Lügen der Kulturmenschheit* (Leipzig: B. Schlicke Verlag, 1884); and David Gross, "Bergson, Proust, and the Revaluation of Memory," *International Philosophical Quarterly* 25 (December 1985): 369–80.

24. On Futurism, see Filippo Marinetti's "Foundations of Futurism" (1909), and on Dadaism, Tristan Tzara's "Dada Manifesto" (1918), both included in *Paths to the Present: Aspects of European Thought from Romanticism to Existentialism*, ed. Eugen Weber (New York: Dodd, Mead, and Co., 1966), pp. 242–53.

25. Charles Baudelaire, "La modernité," *Oeuvres complètes*, ed. Y.-G. Le Dantec, and rev. Claude Pichois (Paris: Éditions Gallimard, 1961), p. 1163.

26. See Erwin Panofsky, *Renaissance and Renascences in Western Art* (Stockholm: Almquist and Wicksel, 1965).

27. Theodor W. Adorno, *Ästhetische Theorie*, in *Gesammelte Schriften*, vol. 7, ed. Gretel Adorno and Rolf Tiedemann (Frankfurt: Suhrkamp, 1972), p. 38.

28. Roger Shattuck, "The Demon of Originality," *The Innocent Eye: On Modern Literature and the Arts* (New York: Farrar, Straus, and Giroux, 1984), pp. 62–81; and Erich Heller, "Karl Kraus," *In the Age of Prose* (Cambridge: Cambridge University Press, 1984), p. 94.

29. Theodor W. Adorno, "Was bedeutet Aufarbeitung der Vergangenheit?" *Erziehung zur Mündigkeit*, ed. G. Kadelbach (Frankfurt: Suhrkamp, 1970), p. 13.

30. It should be added that not all the literary-artistic movements of the period

1880–1920 were modernist, nor were all hostile to tradition. Some revolted backwards and tried to revive earlier cultural traditions which both industrial modernity and aesthetic modernism attacked as obsolete. The German movement of *Heimatkunst* is one such example. Emerging in the 1890s, it was nostalgic for a lost past and longed for a romanticized, traditional community as an alternative to technological emptiness and rootless individualism. After World War I, a fascist version of *Heimatkunst* appeared which eventually replaced the traditional ideal of community with an ecstatic one based on a mystical union with a charismatic leader. See Hamann and Hermann, *Stilkunst um 1900*, pp. 326–47; and Russell Berman, *The Rise of the German Novel* (Cambridge: Harvard University Press, 1986), pp. 205–31.

31. For an overview of these and other aspects of postmodernism, see Andreas Huyssen, *After the Great Divide: Modernism, Mass Culture, Postmodernism* (Bloomington: University of Indiana Press, 1986); Hal Foster, ed., *The Anti-Aesthetic* (Port Townsend: Bay Press, 1983); E. Ann Kaplan, *Postmodernism and Its Discontents* (London: Verso, 1988); Dietmar Kamper and Willem van Reijen, eds., *Der unvollendete Vernunft: Moderne versus Postmoderne* (Frankfurt: Suhrkamp, 1987); Ingeborg Hoesterey, ed., *Zeitgeist in Babel: The Postmodernist Controversy* (Bloomington: University of Indiana Press, 1991); and the special issue of *Theory, Culture and Society* on "Postmodernism," vol. 5 (June 1988).

32. See Gilles Deleuze and Félix Guattari, *Anti-Oedipus: Capitalism and Schizophrenia*, trans. Mark Seem and Helen R. Lane (New York: Viking, 1977); and *Modernes et Après? "Les Immatériaux,"* ed. Élie Théofilakis (Paris: Éditions autrement, 1985).

33. Theodor W. Adorno, *Soziologische Schriften*, in *Gesammelte Werke*, vol. 8, ed. Gretel Adorno and Rolf Tiedemann (Frankfurt: Suhrkamp, 1972), pp. 8, 68, 115.

34. Fredric Jameson, "Postmodernism, or the Cultural Logic of Late Capitalism," *New Left Review* 146 (July-August 1984): 53–92.

4. Survivals and Fabrications

1. One of the assumptions of this position is that wherever tradition rules, a deeper and more authentic kind of experience is possible—one which brings into play the accumulated wisdom of earlier generations. Walter Benjamin developed this point by making a sharp distinction between traditional and modern experience. Traditional experience (*Erfahrung*) is qualitative and unified. Modern experience (*Erlebnis*) is quantative and fragmented. In *Erfahrung*, personal experience is integrated into the community and draws on collective memories. In *Erlebnis*, individual experience is separated from both the community and the collective past; what are called experiences are only sensations which leave no inner residues of meaning that can be built upon. See Walter Benjamin, "On Some Motifs in Baudelaire," in *Illuminations*, trans. Harry Zohn (New York: Schocken, 1969), pp. 163, 186–94.

2. Arnold Gehlen, *Man: His Nature and Place in the World*, trans. Clare McMillan and Karl Pillemer (New York: Columbia University Press, 1988), p. 119.

3. On Gehlen's theory of "relief," see ibid., pp. 21–22, 28–30, 51–52, 57–58, 152, 163. For his theory of social normativity see also Arnold Gehlen, *Moral und Hypermoral: Eine pluralistische Ethik* (Frankfurt: Athenäum Verlag, 1969).

4. On Freud's repetition compulsion, see J. LaPlanche and J.-B. Pontalis, "Compulsion to Repeat (Repetition Compulsion)," in *The Language of Psycho-Analysis*, trans. Donald Nicholson-Smith (London: Hogarth Press, 1973), pp. 78–80.

5. Jürgen Habermas, *Legitimation Crisis*, trans. Thomas McCarthy (Boston: Beacon Press, 1975); see also Claus Offe, " 'Crisis of Crisis Management': Elements of a Political Crisis Theory," in *Contradictions of the Welfare State*, ed. John Keane (Cambridge: MIT Press, 1984), pp. 35–64.

6. Claus Offe, "New Social Movements: Challenges to Boundaries of Institutional Politics," *Social Research* 52, no. 4 (Winter 1985): 819.

7. J.G.A. Pocock, *Politics, Language, and Time: Essays on Political Thought and History* (New York: Atheneum, 1971), p. 80.

8. Traditions of cultural nationalism are of course much older than those of political nationalism; the former date back centuries but the latter only to the eighteenth century. On both forms of nationalism see Friedrich Meinecke, *Cosmopolitanism and the National State*, trans. Robert B. Kimber (Princeton: Princeton University Press, 1970), esp. pp. 9–20; and Anthony D. Smith's two works, *Theories of Nationalism* (New York: Harper and Row, 1971), pp. 153–91; and *The Ethnic Origins of Nations* (New York: Basil Blackwell, 1986), pp. 21–46, 129–52.

9. On this matter see the pertinent essays in Lubomyr Hajda and Mark Beissinger, eds., *The Nationalities Factor in Soviet Politics and Society* (Boulder: Westview Press, 1990); and George Schöpflin, "Nationality in Yugoslav Politics," *Suvey* 25, no. 3 (Summer 1980): 1–19.

10. See Rudolf Braun, *Sozialer und kultureller Wandel in einem ländlichen Industriegebiet im 19. und 20 Jahrhundert* (Erlenbach-Zurich: Zürcher Oberland, 1965); and Eric Hobsbawm, "Introduction: Inventing Traditions," in *The Invention of Tradition*, ed. Eric Hobsbawm and Terence Ranger (Cambridge: Cambridge University Press, 1983), p. 6.

11. Eugen Weber, *Peasants into Frenchmen: The Modernization of Rural France* (Stanford: Stanford University Press, 1976), pp. 377–98, 471–84.

12. The Hobsbawm and Ranger volume (cited above in footnote 10) furnishes several examples of such inventions and fabrications. See also George L. Mosse, "Mass Politics and the Political Liturgy of Nationalism," in *Nationalism: The Nature and Evolution of an Ideal*, ed. Eugene Kamenka (London: St. Martin's Press, 1976), pp. 39–54; and Jean-Pierre Sironneau, *Sécularisation et religions politique* (The Hague: Mouton, 1962), esp. pp. 313–15.

13. Louis Dimier, *Les maitres de la contre-révolution au dix-neuvième siècle* (Paris: Nouvelle librairie nationale, 1917).

14. This at least was the case up until the 1940s. In the first two decades of its existence, the Soviet state saw nothing in the Russian past to which it wanted to be linked. To the Bolsheviks particularly, tradition simply meant the tradition of serfdom and autocracy. Hence, in place of any kind of interest in the "old," the focus was almost entirely on the "new," i.e., the new man, the new society, the

new economy. El Lissitzky's four-step approach to social change was typical of the whole Soviet mood after 1917; it called for the *negation* of all antagonistic forms of life and thought, the *propagation* of a classless society, the *destruction* of all life-negating remnants, and finally the *construction* of a "new life environment in the free space created by the Revolution." See Eric Dluhosch, "The Failure of the Soviet Avant-garde," *Oppositions* 10 (Fall 1977): 36–37. Marx, it should be noted, had a less extreme view of how to relate to tradition. Despite his apparent hostility to tradition in *The Eighteenth Brumaire* ("the tradition of all the dead generations weighs like a nightmare on the brain of the living"), Marx actually advocated a "critical appropriation" of the best of the past. In some of his works, he distinguished between progressive and regressive traditions; the latter were to be rejected, but the former needed to be brought to fruition. (Here he especially had in mind progressive *bürgerlich* traditions, e.g., those which promoted the "ideals" of liberty, equality, and fraternity, but which had not advanced far enough to embody these ideals in practice.) Obviously Marx, like the Soviets, completely rejected the notion that traditions ought to be "invented." But unlike them he believed that certain traditions should be "completed"—that is, moved out of the realm of ideas and into the realm of social action. On Marx's view of tradition see Alois Hönig, "Zur geschichtsphilosophischen Kategorie Tradition," *Deutsche Zeitschrift für Philosophie* 12, no. 1 (1964): 1055–72.

15. See William Leiss, Stephen Kline, and Sut Jhally, *Social Communication in Advertising* (New York: Methuen, 1986), pp. 11–12, 210–15, 237–46.

16. As Roland Marchand has convincingly shown, the primary task of advertising is still to integrate the consumer fully into modernity, i.e., to make him or her eager to embrace new products, new technologies, new "lifestyles." But at the same time advertisers have not remained indifferent to the loss of the past which modernity entails. Hence they have also tried to appeal in every way possible to the lingering and still very powerful need for tradition. See Roland Marchand, *Advertising and the American Dream: Making Way for Modernity, 1920–1940* (Berkeley: University of California Press, 1985), pp. xxi, 13, 359–60. For a very different point of view—namely, that advertising is "mythic" and therefore performs a conservative function in contemporary life—see Varda Langholz Leymore, *Hidden Myth: Structures and Symbolism in Advertising* (New York: Basic Books, 1975).

17. See Jean-François Lyotard, *Économie libidinale* (Paris: Éditions de minuit, 1974). In the 1920s, Ludwig Klages made a similar point about images reaching down to the "soul," but representations touching only the "mind." See Ludwig Klages, *Der Geist als Widersacher der Seele* (Leipzig: J. A. Barth, 1929); and Walter Benjamin, "Johann Jakob Bachofen," *Gesammelte Schriften* vol. 2, no. 1, ed. Rolf Tiedemann and Hermann Schweppenhäuser (Frankfurt: Suhrkamp, 1977), pp. 229–30.

18. A distinction needs to be made between ancient and modern nostalgia. Ancient nostalgia, of the kind found in writings extending from the time of Homer to the seventeenth century and beyond, meant primarily a longing for home, or "homesickness." This was the *nostos*—the "yearning to return"—that Homer described in Ulysses when, in his wanderings, Ulysses fondly remem-

bered Ithaca. It is what the Jews felt during the Babylonian Captivity ("By the waters of Babylon we sat and wept when we remembered Zion"). It was the sentiment Dante experienced around 1300 A.D. when, in exile, he recalled the beauties of Florence. And it was the feeling that gripped Swiss mercenaries in the late 1600s when, far from home, they reminisced about the alpine valleys of their native land. (The word "nostalgia" itself was coined in 1688 by the Swiss physician Johannes Hofer, who wrote a medical dissertation on the subject.) In the last couple of centuries, however, the word has acquired a somewhat different meaning. Now it denotes not so much a longing for another *place* (though it can still mean that, too) as a longing for another *time*. Hence, instead of carrying primarily spatial references, "modern" nostalgia more often carries temporal ones, as is evident in the Romantics' nostalgia for the Middle Ages, or in Proust's nostalgia for earlier moments in his own life. See Johannes Hofer, "Medical Dissertation on Nostalgia," trans. by Carolyn K. Anspach, *Bulletin of the History of Medicine* 2 (1934): 374–91; Edward S. Casey, "The World of Nostalgia," *Man and World* 20 (1987): 361–84; and Donald M. Lowe, *History of Bourgeois Perception* (Chicago: University of Chicago Press, 1982), pp. 40–41.

19. For a more extensive discussion of the qualities of nostalgia, consult especially Fred Davis, *Yearning for Yesterday: A Sociology of Nostalgia* (New York: Free Press, 1979); and James Hart, "Toward a Phenomenology of Nostalgia," *Man and World* 6 (1973): 397–420.

20. On this process, see David Lowenthal, *The Past Is a Foreign Country* (New York: Cambridge University Press, 1985), pp. 324ff.; and Fred Davis, *Yearning for Yesterday*, pp. 118–22, 125–27.

5. Rethinking Tradition

1. Gianni Vattimo, *The End of Modernity: Nihilism and Hermeneutics in Postmodern Culture*, trans. Jon R. Snyder (Baltimore: Johns Hopkins University Press, 1988), pp. li, 176–80.

2. On traditionalism, see John Kautsky, *The Political Consequences of Modernization* (New York: Wiley, 1972), pp. 101–6; S. N. Eisenstadt, "Some Observations on the Dynamics of Tradition," *Comparative Studies in Society and History* 11, no. 4 (October 1969): 462–66; and S. N. Eisenstadt, "Continuity and Reconstruction of Tradition," *Post-Traditional Societies* (New York: Norton, 1974), pp. 22ff.

3. Klaus Bergmann, *Agrarromantik und Grossstadtfeindschaft* (Meisenheim: Verlag Anton Hain, 1970), pp. 33–102.

4. Hobsbawm has gone so far as to say that "in a sense, the rise of the Nazi Party in Germany . . . was the last genuine mass movement of peasants at least in the Protestant parts of Germany." Eric Hobsbawm, "Peasants and Politics," *Journal of Peasant Studies* 1, no. 1 (1973): 20.

5. Historicism was not a "school" of history, but rather a way of seeing or thinking about the historical past. Philosophically its roots went back (at least in Germany) to Möser and Herder in the eighteenth century. Under their influence, historians not only began looking more carefully at the cultural uniqueness and

particularity of the past, but they also tried to express in their work the rich "inner spirit" of earlier traditions and epochs. For the main characteristics of historicism see Friedrich Meinecke, *Historism: The Rise of a New Historical Outlook,* trans. J. E. Anderson (London: Routledge and Kegan Paul, 1972), pp. 235–495.

6. Leopold von Ranke, cited in Leonard Krieger, *The Meaning of History* (Chicago: University of Chicago Press, 1977), p. 361.

7. Yosef Yerushalmi has skillfully delineated the process by which Jewish historiography over the last century and a half has separated itself from the traditions of Jewish collective memory. The latter had always been conveyed by rituals, liturgies, public readings, and the like, but not by formal recorded history. I believe a similar process has occurred on a broader scale within Western secular history. See Yosef Hayim Yerushalmi, *Zakhor: Jewish History and Jewish Memory* (Seattle and London: University of Washington Press, 1982), pp. 39–46, 86, 91–103.

8. See my essay "Temporality and the Modern State," *Theory and Society* 14 (1985): 68–70.

9. This quote is from Fredric Jameson, "Marxism and Historicism," *New Literary History* 11, no. 1 (Autumn, 1979): 44. For some sense of the radical difference of archaic traditions, see inter alia E. R. Dodds, *The Greeks and the Irrational* (Berkeley: University of California Press, 1951); Walter Burkert, *Greek Religion,* trans. John Raffan (Cambridge: Harvard University Press, 1985); and Jean-Pierre Vernant, *Myth and Thought among the Greeks* (London: Routledge and Kegan Paul, 1983).

10. The term is Russell Berman's. For an excellent brief description of how otherness is culturally co-opted, see his "Modern Art and Desublimation," *Telos* 62 (Winter 1984–85): 31–57.

11. The rather antiquated word *unheimisch*—used here as the antonym of *heimisch* (meaning "native," or "homey")—needs to be distinguished from the more familiar *unheimlich,* which is usually translated as "uncanny," "sinister," or "gloomy." It is this latter term, for example, that Freud used in his famous essay of 1919 on "the uncanny" (*"Das Unheimliche"*).

12. On Hölderlin's views see his letter to Casimir Ulrich Böhlendorff, December 4, 1801, in *Briefe,* ed. Adolf Beck, in *Friedrich Hölderlin: Samtliche Werke,* gen. ed. Friedrich Beissner, vol. 6 (Stuttgart: Kohlhammer Verlag, 1954), pp. 425–28; and Richard Sieburth, "Introduction," *Friedrich Hölderlin, Hymns and Fragments* (Princeton: Princeton University Press, 1984), pp. 11–16.

13. Clifford Geertz, "The Uses of Diversity," *Michigan Quarterly Review* 25, no. 1 (Winter 1986): 118.

14. See Jürgen Habermas, "The Dialectics of Rationalization: An Interview with Jürgen Habermas," *Telos* 49 (Fall 1981): 28.

6. Reappropriating Tradition through Its Traces

1. Notable in this regard (to stay only with the nineteenth century) is the work of John Roby and George Laurence Gomme in England, Paul Sébillot and Frédéric Noëlas in France, and W. H. Riehl in Germany (the individual generally credited with founding the modern study of *Volkskunde*).

2. For an excellent discussion of how this reconstitution has occurred, see Hermann Bausinger, *Folk Culture in a World of Technology*, trans. Elke Dettmer (Bloomington and Indianapolis: Indiana University Press, 1990).

3. See Wilhelm Pinder, *Das Problem der Generationen in der Kunstgeschichte Europas* (Berlin: Frankfurter Verlags-Anstalt, 1926), pp. 67–69; Karl Mannheim, "Das Problem des Generationen," in *Wissenssoziologie*, ed. Kurt H. Wolff (Berlin and Neuwied: Luchterhand, 1964), pp. 517, 521; Ernst Bloch, *Erbschaft dieser Zeit* (Frankfurt: Suhrkamp, 1985; 1st ed., 1935), pp. 104–26; and Ernst Bloch, "Über Ungleichzeitigkeit, Provinz, und Propaganda: Ein Gespräch mit Rainer Traub und Harald Wieser," *Gespräche mit Ernst Bloch*, ed. Rainer Traub and Harald Wieser (Frankfurt: Suhrkamp, 1975), pp. 196–207.

4. These examples come from Umberto Eco, "Function and Sign: The Semiotics of Architecture," in *Signs, Symbols, and Architecture*, ed. Geoffrey Broadbent, Richard Bunt, and Charles Jencks (Chichester and New York: John Wiley & Sons, 1980), pp. 28–29.

5. The moral courage displayed by the French villagers of Le Chambon during the time of the Nazi occupation of France is a case in point. To a considerable extent their collective efforts to save the Jews at great risk to themselves came from seemingly "unmodern" survivals of Huguenot beliefs and convictions dating back to the sixteenth century. See Philip P. Hallie, *Lest Innocent Blood Be Shed* (New York: Harper and Row, 1975).

6. Weber argued this position only in the early 1890s. By 1894 he had changed his mind about the traditional German aristocracy, and more particularly the East Elbian Junkers who were his main concern. Now it appeared to Weber that the aristocracy had given up its ideals, gone over to a petty bourgeois frame of mind, and started to adopt materialistic and vulgarly commercial attitudes. In other words, he faulted them for abandoning a noncontemporaneous *Lebenstil* in order to acquire a thoroughly modern one. See Arthur Mitzman, *The Iron Cage: An Historical Interpretation of Max Weber* (New Brunswick: Transaction Books, 1985), pp. 122–26; and Wilhelm Hennis, *Max Weber: Essays in Reconstruction*, trans. Keith Tribe (London and Boston: Allen and Unwin, 1988), pp. 76–78.

7. See Henri Lefebvre, *Everyday Life in the Modern World*, trans. Sacha Rabinovitch (New York: Harper and Row, 1971), pp. 111–42.

8. See my essay "Critical Synthesis on Urban Knowledge: Remembering and Forgetting in the Modern City," *Social Epistemology* 4, no. 1 (1990): 3–22.

9. Heinrich Heine, cited in Lucien Goldmann, *Immanuel Kant* (London: New Left Books, 1971), p. 44.

10. Walter Benjamin, *Illuminations*, trans. Harry Zohn (New York: Schocken, 1969), pp. 220–21. For his own reasons, Benjamin approved of this shattering of tradition, but that is not the issue here.

11. Ibid., p. 222.

12. Fredric Jameson, *The Political Unconscious* (Ithaca: Cornell University Press, 1981), p. 19.

13. Incidentally, the point of juxtaposition would *not* be to bring only the "good" of the past forward and leave the "bad" behind. To be effective, judgments

of any kind would have to be avoided, since they are likely to be made on the basis of a contemporary system of values. This would color the past rather than let it speak for itself on its own terms. For the juxtapositional method it is simply tradition *as such* that needs to be contacted, and it is a secondary question whether that tradition is good or bad according to modern opinion. What counts is strictly tradition's potential to disturb. The key is that a reaction of unsettlement occur. The unsettlement can be, and usually is, mental or intellectual, but it can just as well be emotional (e.g., awe, wonder, excitement; or revulsion, loathing, nausea). In truth, there is a whole gamut of legitimate responses to otherness. All that matters in the method that I am describing here is that some kind of powerful response be provoked—a response powerful enough to raise basic questions about the unexamined *donnés* of modern life. On this see Fredric Jameson, "Marxism and Historicism," *New Literary History* 11, no. 1 (Fall 1979): 55.

14. The *veillées* were winter gatherings of families and neighbors lasting roughly from dusk to midnight which dated back at least to the Middle Ages. They appear to have originated out of the need to save on heat by sharing it, but over time the *veillées* began to serve a number of other functions as well. To mention only a few, they provided the occasion for communal singing and storytelling, the passing on of skills from old to young, the reinforcement of village precepts, and the recitation of lore about distant ancestors. Nevertheless, despite their long history, the *veillées* were in full decline by the 1880s. After World War I, they became defunct largely due to the transformative impact of modernity (e.g., new roads, more mobility, easier access to urban centers, the turn toward privatization, etc.). See Eugen Weber, *Peasants into Frenchmen: The Modernization of Rural France, 1870–1914* (Stanford: Stanford University Press, 1976), pp. 413–18.

15. The phrase is the historian Johann Gustav Droysen's, cited in Hans-Georg Gadamer, *Truth and Method*, trans. Garrett Barden and John Cumming (New York: Crossroad, 1965), p. 349.

16. Theodore Kisiel, "The Happening of Tradition: The Hermeneutics of Gadamer and Heidegger," *Man and World* 2, no. 3 (1969): 363. True, the text still has to be *interpreted* in the present. Hence, even if the text belongs wholly to the past which produced it, its meanings and significations are nevertheless always *received* by a contemporary reader who may comprehend them differently than their author would have wanted. Just as no work is ever written in a pure state (i.e., detached from its surroundings), so too there is no such thing as a pure reader, free from the assumptions and presuppositions of his age.

17. Gadamer discusses at length the conservative nature of language, including the way it preserves the "meaning worlds" of the past in its words and metaphors, even in its grammar and syntax. Though this discussion is important for Gadamer's philosophical hermeneutics, it is not necessary to pursue it here. See Gadamer, *Truth and Method*, pp. 345–447.

18. Joel C. Weinsheimer, *Gadamer's Hermeneutics: A Reading of "Truth and Method"* (New Haven: Yale University Press, 1985), p. 251.

19. Gadamer, *Truth and Method*, p. 348.

20. Hans-Georg Gadamer, "The Problem of Historical Consciousness," in *Interpretive Social Science*, ed. Paul Rabinow and William W. Sullivan (Berkeley: University of California Press, 1979), p. 108.

21. Friedrich Nietzsche, *The Gay Science*, trans. Walter Kaufmann (New York: Vintage, 1974), p. 300.

22. Gadamer, *Truth and Method*, pp. 269–74, 337–41.

23. Ibid., pp. 351, 420. In a later work Gadamer argued even more broadly that "reality happens precisely *within* language." Hans-Georg Gadamer, "On the Scope and Function of Hermeneutical Reflection," *Continuum* 8, nos. 1–2 (Spring-Summer 1970): 90.

24. For example, there are traditions of taste, class attitude, ethnic prejudice, and the like that are never put into words, but which nonetheless exist as part of the warp and woof of everyday life. Pierre Bourdieu discusses some of these traditions in his *Distinction: A Social Critique of the Judgement of Taste*, trans. Richard Nice (Cambridge: Harvard University Press), pp. 11–96, 260–317. See also Maurice Halbwachs, *Les cadres sociaux de la mémoire* (Paris: Presses universitaires de France, 1952), pp. 146–77, 222–72.

25. See Jürgen Habermas, "A Review of Gadamer's *Truth and Method*," in *Understanding and Social Inquiry*, ed. Fred R. Dallmayr and Thomas A. McCarthy (Notre Dame: Notre Dame University Press, 1977), p. 361; and Karl-Otto Apel, ed., *Hermeneutik and Ideologiekritik* (Frankfurt: Suhrkamp, 1970).

26. The suggestion that there might be a "decline of hearing" today should of course not be taken physiologically. Rather, it should be related to what may be a general decline in the *capacity to listen*, which in turn may be due to a withering of oral traditions, and of the "communit[ies] of listeners" such traditions entail. (According to a hypothesis of Walter Benjamin's, when people no longer share collective aural experiences, the "gift for listening" atrophies because it lacks reinforcement from the larger social community. See Benjamin, "The Storyteller," *Illuminations*, pp. 83–109; and Andrew Benjamin, "Tradition and Experience: Walter Benjamin's 'On Some Motifs in Baudelaire,'" in *Problems of Modernity: Adorno and Benjamin*, ed. Andrew Benjamin (London and New York: Routledge, 1989), pp. 91, 124, 128, 134.

7. Subversive Genealogy

1. For Bloch's views on *Umfunktionierung*, see *Erbschaft dieser Zeit* (Frankfurt: Suhrkamp, 1985), pp. 111–26, 225–28; for Brecht's use of this term, see the discussion in Heinz Brüggemann, *Literarische Technik und soziale Revolution* (Reinbek: Rowohlt, 1973), pp. 147–77, 234–47, 268–74.

2. In Chapter 6, I dealt *only* with the gradual refunctioning that happens to those fragments of tradition that have managed to survive after the disappearance of the traditions of which they were once a part. Over decades or generations these fragments are rearranged in new contexts and eventually take on new meanings; but this process happens almost offhandedly, and without the calculated support of outside interests.

3. Walter Benjamin, "Anmerkungen zu 'Über den Begriff des Geschichte,'"

Gesammelte Schriften, vol. 1, no. 3, ed. Rolf Tiedemann and Hermann Schweppenhäuser (Frankfurt: Suhrkamp, 1974), 1242–43; Susan Buck-Morss, "Walter Benjamin—Revolutionary Writer (I)," *New Left Review* 126 (July-August 1981): 56.

4. See Jack Zipes, *Breaking the Magic Spell: Radical Theories of Folk and Fairy Tales* (Austin: University of Texas Press, 1979), pp. 105, 112–17.

5. Jean Baudrillard has pushed this argument the furthest by claiming that even the concept of "the real" no longer has meaning. Reality has been superseded by "hyperreality." See Jean Baudrillard, *Simulations,* trans. Paul Foss, Paul Patton, and Philip Beitchman (New York: Semiotext(e), 1983), pp. 23–49, 138–52.

6. Jacques Derrida, "Letter to a Japanese Friend," in *Derrida and Différance,* ed. David Wood and Robert Bernasconi (Evanston: Northwestern University Press, 1988), p. 3.

7. Jonathan Culler, *On Deconstruction: Theory and Criticism after Structuralism* (Ithaca: Cornell University Press, 1982), pp. 140, 148, 150.

8. Over the past two decades, Derrida has written very little commentary on social or cultural experiences, and most of his closest followers have not either (Paul de Man, J. Hillis Miller, Geoffrey Hartman, etc.). However, other deconstructionists (Michael Ryan, Gayatri Chakravorty Spivak, Teresa de Lauretis, etc.) have drawn on Derrida to develop a variety of Marxist and/or feminist forms of deconstruction which have addressed larger social and political issues.

9. It is worth noting, however, that some deconstructionists have argued that play, far from avoiding critique, can in fact be one of the most effective forms of critique. See Mark C. Taylor, *Altarity* (Chicago: University of Chicago Press, 1987); James Ogilvy, *Many Dimensional Man: Decentralizing Self, Society, and the Sacred* (New York: Oxford, 1977); and Gregory Ulmer, *Applied Grammatology* (Baltimore: Johns Hopkins University Press, 1985).

10. Burr C. Bundage, "The Birth of Clio: A Résumé and Interpretation of Ancient Near Eastern Historiography," in *Teachers of History,* ed. H. Stuart Hughes (Ithaca: Cornell University Press, 1954), pp. 200–210.

11. Bernhard A. Groningen, *In the Grip of the Past: An Essay on Greek Thought* (Leiden: E. J. Brill, 1953), pp. 47–61.

12. See Gerd Tellenbach, "Vom karolingischen Reichsadel zum deutschen Reichsfürstenstand," *Herrschaft und Staat in Mittelalter* (Darmstadt: Wege der Forschung, ii, 1956); Karl Ferdinand Werner, "Untersuchungen zur Frühzeit des französischen Fürstentums (9.-10. Jahrhundert)," *Die Welt als Geschichte* 17 (1958): 256–89; 19 (1959): 146–93; 20 (1960): 87–119; K. Leyser, "The German Aristocracy from the Ninth to the Early Twelfth Century," *Past and Present,* no. 41 (December, 1968): 25–53; and Georges Duby, "French Genealogical Literature: The Eleventh and Twelfth Centuries," *The Chivalrous Society,* trans. Cynthia Postan (Berkeley: University of California Press, 1977), pp. 149–57.

13. Hobbes and Kant cited in Judith Shklar, "Subversive Genealogies," *Daedalus* 101 (Winter 1972): 129.

14. See especially Nietzsche's *The Use and Abuse of History,* trans. Adrian Collins (Indianapolis: Bobbs-Merrill, 1957). On the various kinds of genealogies and Nietzsche's relation to them, see Mark Warren, *Nietzsche and Political Thought* (Cambridge: MIT Press, 1988), pp. 102–10. In the last decade of his

productive life Nietzsche also addressed the problem of "nihilism" (i.e., the danger of *too much* release from tradition).

15. It is of course also true that differences can be distinguished between what a tradition was *ab origine,* and what it became historically. Since all traditions undergo modifications in the process of being passed down, they naturally look different after a series of transmissions than they did at the beginning. But so long as these modifications take place *within* a continuous tradition, and above all within a framework of respect for the tradition, they do not destroy the integrity of what they modify. A healthy "play" exists between what a tradition was at first and what it becomes later. However, this is not what happens when a tradition is refunctioned. In a refunctioning process all or part of a tradition may be formally preserved, but always at the cost of being taken outside itself, reassembled, and used against its own initial spirit or intent. For this reason, a refunctioning is a far more damaging event in a tradition's history than is a modification or embellishment.

16. Ernst Bloch, "Zur Originalgeschichte des Dritten Reiches," in *Erbschaft dieser Zeit,* pp. 126–52.

17. See Bloch's chapter on noncontemporaneity in ibid., pp. 104–26.

8. The Tactics of Tradition

1. With regard to Poland, for example, Czeslaw Milosz has pointed out the importance of historical memory for Polish collective identity. (See Czeslaw Milosz, "An Interview with Czeslaw Milosz," *New York Review of Books,* Feb. 17, 1986, pp. 34–35.) Milan Kundera has made a similar point about Central Europe in general. (See Milan Kundera, "The Tragedy of Central Europe," *New York Review of Books,* April 26, 1984, pp. 33–39.)

2. John Armstrong, "The Ethnic Scene in the Soviet Union: The View of the Dictatorship," *Journal of Soviet Nationalities* 1, no. 1 (Spring 1990): 15.

3. By the "republican tradition" I mean the centuries-old legacy of thought and practice in the West which stresses, among other things, the importance of "civic virtue" (i.e., political involvement and responsibility) as a primary value, and which therefore elevates the "public weal" to a position far above the merely private realm of individual self-interest. Because of its rejection of possessive individualism and its hostility to interest group politics, the republican tradition has not found a place for itself at the center of twentieth-century political life. On the main tenets of this tradition see J.G.A. Pocock, *The Machiavellian Moment: Florentine Political Thought and the Atlantic Republican Tradition* (Princeton: Princeton University Press, 1975); for its marginal status in the West today see William M. Sullivan, *Reconstructing Public Philosophy* (Berkeley: University of California Press, 1982).

4. Norman Cohn, *Pursuit of the Millennium* (New York: Harper and Row, 1961), pp. 149–94. The Brethren of the Free Spirit survived in Central Europe for some 400 years (between approximately 1200 and 1600 A.D.), passing on their literature in secret and practicing their beliefs in small groups despite the efforts of the Catholic Church and the German states to eradicate them.

5. Rabbinical Judaism was a tradition of the margins, because it existed for centuries in the open but at the fringes of society (e.g., in urban ghettos, village *shtetls*, etc.). Nevertheless, within Judaism itself there were extremist Kabbalistic and eschatological traditions which challenged the Judaism of the Torah. These rebellious traditions took refuge underground and were naturally condemned as subversive by Orthodox Judaism. See Gershom Scholem, *Sabbatai Sevi: The Mystical Messiah, 1626–1676,* trans. R.J.Z. Werblowsky (Princeton: Princeton University Press, 1973); and "Toward an Understanding of the Messianic Idea in Judaism," *The Messianic Idea in Judaism* (New York: Schocken, 1971), pp. 1–36.

6. See Hannah Arendt, *On Revolution* (New York: Viking, 1968), p. 252.

7. The terms "tactics" and "strategy" are defined and discussed in Michel de Certeau, *The Practices of Everyday Life,* trans. Steven F. Rendall (Berkeley: University of California Press, 1984), pp. xvii–xx, 24–42. However, my definitions differ somewhat from de Certeau's, since for him tactics are mainly an art of "using time," and strategies a way of "occupying space."

8. Ibid., p. xix.

9. Many of the traditions that stay at or near the center retain their outward forms but let go of their original contents. On the other hand, there are also traditions that keep their original contents while letting go of their outward forms (e.g., the seemingly antiquated religious traditions which continue on as explicit themes in modern secular films or novels). See Jean-Pierre Sironneau, *Sécularisation et religions politique* (The Hague: Mouton, 1962), pp. 188–96.

10. During the period of Roman persecutions from the first to the fourth centuries A.D., the tenets of Christianity were passed on mainly orally—through preaching or personal contact. The Bible was of course a central text, but other than that, there was a great paucity of Christian writing during this time, though there were numerous iconic inscriptions to represent the key ideas of Christianity to the initiated. See Ramsay MacMullen, *Christianity and the Roman Empire (A.D. 100–400)* (New Haven: Yale University Press, 1984), pp. 102, 111. On the secret transmission of traditions, see Leo Strauss, *Persecution and the Art of Writing* (Glencoe: The Free Press, 1952); and Hans Speier, "The Communication of Hidden Meaning," in *Propaganda and Communication in World History,* ed. Harold D. Lasswell, Daniel Lerner, and Hans Speier (Honolulu: University of Hawaii Press, 1980), pp. 261–300.

11. Certeau, *Practices,* p. 1.

12. On symbolic traditions see Herbert Gans, "Symbolic Ethnicity: The Future of Ethnic Groups and Cultures in America," *Ethnic and Racial Studies* 2, no. 1 (January 1979): 1–20; and Richard D. Alba, *Ethnic Identity: The Transformation of White America* (New Haven: Yale University Press, 1990), pp. 75–105, 290–310.

9. Conclusion

1. In saying this, I want to be clear that modernity is not the same as modernism, nor is postmodernity identical with postmodernism. Thus, it is possible to

argue (as I do in Chapter 3) that postmodernism has replaced modernism as our "cultural dominant," and yet reject the notion that postmodernity has replaced modernity as our dominant *social* reality.

2. See Jean Baudrillard's comments in "On Nihilism," *On the Beach* 6 (Spring 1984): 24–25; cited in Douglas Kellner, "Postmodernism as Social Theory," *Theory, Culture and Society* 5, nos. 2–3 (June 1988): 247–48.

3. For an extremely interesting discussion of immanent critique, total critique, and the "redemptive paradigm," see the following recent articles and essays: Richard Wolin, "Utopia, Mimesis, and Reconciliation: A Redemptive Critique of Adorno's *Aesthetic Theory*," *Representations* 32 (Fall 1990): 33–49; Anson Rabinbach, "Benjamin, Bloch and Modern German Jewish Messianism," *New German Critique* 34 (Winter 1985): 78–124; Ferenc Feher, "Redemptive and Democratic Paradigms in Radical Politics," *Telos* 63 (Spring 1985): 147–56; Joel Whitebook, "The Politics of Redemption," *Telos* 63 (Spring 1985): 156–68; Paul Breines, "Redeeming Redemption," *Telos* 65 (Fall 1985): 152–58; Richard Wolin, "Against Adjustment," *Telos* 65 (Fall 1985): 158–63; and Moishe Gonzales, "Theoretical Amnesia," *Telos* 65 (Fall 1985): 163–70.

4. Wolin, "Against Adjustment," p. 161.

5. Marshall Berman, *All That Is Solid Melts into Air: The Experience of Modernity* (New York: Simon and Shuster, 1982), p. 36.

Bibliography

Adorno, Theodor W. *Ästhetische Theorie.* In *Gesammelte Werke,* vol. 7. Edited by Gretel Adorno and Rolf Tiedemann. Frankfurt: Suhrkamp, 1972.

————. *Soziologische Schriften.* In *Gesammelte Werke,* vol. 8. Edited by Gretel Adorno and Rolf Tiedemann. Frankfurt: Suhrkamp, 1972.

————. "Was bedeutet Aufarbeitung der Vergangenheit?" *Erziehung zur Mündigkeit.* Edited by G. Kadelbach. Frankfurt: Suhrkamp, 1970.

Alba, Richard D. *Ethnic Identity: The Transformation of White America.* New Haven: Yale University Press, 1990.

Anchor, Robert. *The Enlightenment Tradition.* New York: Harper and Row, 1967.

Anderson, Perry. *Lineages of the Absolutist State.* London: New Left Books, 1974.

Apel, Karl-Otto, ed. *Hermeneutik und Ideologiekritik.* Frankfurt: Suhrkamp, 1970.

Arendt, Hannah. *On Revolution.* New York: Viking, 1968.

Ariès, Philippe. "Confessions d'un anarchiste de droite." *Contrepoint* 16 (1975): 87–89.

Armstrong, John. "The Ethnic Scene in the Soviet Union: The View of the Dictatorship." *Journal of Soviet Studies* 1, no. 1 (Spring 1990): 14–65.

Bacon, Francis. *The Works of Francis Bacon,* vol. 4. Edited by James Spedding, R. L. Ellis, and D. D. Heath. London: Longmans and Co., 1883.

Baczko, Bronislaw. "Die französische Aufklärung und die Philosophie des Konkreten." *Weltanschauung, Metaphysik, Entfremdung: Philosophische Versuche.* Frankfurt: Suhrkamp, 1969.

Baudelaire, Charles. "La modernité." *Oeuvres complètes.* Edited by Y.-G. Le Dantec. Revised by Claude Pichois. Paris: Éditions Gallimard, 1961.

Baudrillard, Jean. *Simulations.* Translated by Paul Foss, Paul Patton, and Philip Beitchman. New York: Semiotext(e), 1983.

Bausinger, Hermann. *Folk Culture in a World of Technology.* Translated by Elke Dettmer. Bloomington and Indianapolis: Indiana University Press, 1990.

Beierwaltes, Werner. "Subjektivität, Schöpfertum, Freiheit: Die Philosophie der Renaissance zwischen Tradition und neuzeitlichem Bewusstsein." In *Der Übergang zur Neuzeit und die Wirkung von Traditionen.* Papers presented to the Joachim Jungius-Gesellschaft. Göttingen: Vandenhoeck und Ruprecht, 1978.

Beik, William. *Absolutism and Society in Seventeenth-Century France.* Cambridge: Cambridge University Press, 1985.

Belperron, Pierre. *La Croisade contre Les Albigeois.* Paris: Librairie Plon, 1948.

Benhabib, Seyla. "Modernity and the Aporias of Critical Theory." *Telos* 49 (Fall 1981): 36–60.

Benjamin, Andrew. "Tradition and Experience: Walter Benjamin's 'On Some Motifs in Baudelaire.'" In *Problems of Modernity: Adorno and Benjamin,* edited by Andrew Benjamin. London and New York: Routledge, 1989.

Benjamin, Walter. "Anmerkungen zu 'Über den Begriff des Geschichte.'" *Gesammelte Schriften,* vol. 1, no. 3. Edited by Rolf Tiedemann and Hermann Schweppenhäuser. Frankfurt: Suhrkamp, 1974.

———. "Johann Jakob Bachofen." *Gesammelte Schriften,* vol. 2, no. 1. Edited by Rolf Tiedemann and Hermann Schweppenhäuser. Frankfurt: Suhrkamp, 1977.

———. *Illuminations.* Translated by Harry Zohn. New York: Schocken, 1969.

Berger, Peter. *Facing Up to Modernity.* New York: Basic Books, 1977.

Bergmann, Klaus. *Agrarromantik und Grossstadtfeindschaft.* Meisenheim: Verlag Anton Hain, 1970.

Berman, Marshall. *All That Is Solid Melts into Air.* New York: Simon and Schuster, 1982.

Berman, Russell. "Modern Art and Desublimation." *Telos* 62 (Winter 1984–85): 31–57.

———. *The Rise of the German Novel.* Cambridge: Harvard University Press, 1986.

Bloch, Ernst. *Erbschaft dieser Zeit.* Frankfurt: Suhrkamp, 1985.

———. "Über Ungleichzeitigkeit, Provinz, und Propaganda." In *Gespräche mit Ernst Bloch,* edited by Rainer Traub and Harald Wieser. Frankfurt: Suhrkamp, 1975.

Blumenberg, Hans. *The Legitimacy of the Modern Age.* Translated by Robert M. Wallace. Cambridge: MIT Press, 1983.

Böhme, Hartmut, and Gernot Böhme. *Das Andere der Vernunft.* Frankfurt: Suhrkamp, 1983.

Boillot, Félix. *Du culte de la tradition.* Paris: Les Presses universitaires de France, 1927.

Bollnow, O. F. *Die Lebensphilosophie.* Berlin: Springer-Verlag, 1958.

Bourdieu, Pierre. *Distinction: A Social Critique of the Judgement of Taste.* Translated by Richard Nice. Cambridge: Harvard University Press, 1984.

Boyer, Christine. *Dreaming the Rational City.* Cambridge: MIT Press, 1983.

Braun, Rudolf. *Sozialer und kultureller Wandel in einem ländlichen Industriegebiet im 19. und 20. Jahrhundert.* Erlenbach-Zurich: Zurcher Oberland, 1965.

Breines, Paul. "Redeeming Redemption." *Telos* 65 (Fall 1985): 152–58.

Brüggemann, Heinz. *Literarische Technik und sociale Revolution.* Reinbek: Rowohlt, 1973.

Buck-Morss, Susan. "Semiotic Boundaries and the Politics of Meaning: Modernity on Tour—A Village in Transition." In *New Ways of Knowing: The Sciences, Society, and Reconstructive Knowledge*, edited by Marcus G. Raskin and Herbert J. Bernstein. Towata: Rowman and Littlefield, 1987.

———. "Walter Benjamin—Revolutionary Writer (I)." *New Left Review* 126 (July-August 1981): 50–75.

Bundage, Burr C. "The Birth of Clio: A Resumé and Interpretation of Ancient Near Eastern Historiography." In *Teachers of History*, edited by H. Stuart Hughes. Ithaca: Cornell University Press, 1954.

Burke, Edmund. *Reflections on the Revolution in France*. Edited by Willam B. Todd. New York: Rinehart and Co., 1959.

Burkert, Walter. *Greek Religion*. Translated by John Raffan. Cambridge: Harvard University Press, 1985.

Casey, Edward S. "The World of Nostalgia." *Man and World* 20 (1987): 361–84.

Certeau, Michel de. *The Practices of Everyday Life*. Translated by Steven F. Rendall. Berkeley: University of California Press, 1984.

Chapman, Raymond. *The Sense of the Past in Victorian Literature*. New York: St. Martin's Press, 1986.

Clanchy, M. T. *From Memory to Written Record: England, 1066–1307*. Cambridge: Harvard University Press, 1979.

Clifford, James. *The Predicament of Culture*. Cambridge: Harvard University Press, 1988.

Cohn, Norman. *Pursuit of the Millennium*. New York: Harper and Row, 1961.

Congar, Yves. *The Meaning of Tradition*. Translated by A. N. Woodrow. New York: Hawthorn Books, 1964.

Culler, Jonathan. *On Deconstruction: Theory and Criticism after Structuralism*. Ithaca: Cornell University Press, 1982.

Dandeker, Christopher. *Surveillance, Power and Modernity: Bureaucracy and Discipline from 1700 to the Present Day*. New York: St. Martin's Press, 1990.

Davis, Fred. *Yearning for Yesterday: A Sociology of Nostalgia*. New York: Free Press, 1979.

Deleuze, Gilles, and Félix Guattari. *Anti-Oedipus: Capitalism and Schizophrenia*. Translated by Mark Seem and Helen R. Lane. New York: Viking, 1977.

Denzer, Horst. *Moralphilosophie und Naturrecht bei Samuel Pufendorf*. Munich: Verlag C. H. Beck, 1972.

Derrida, Jacques. "Letter to a Japanese Friend." In *Derrida and Différance*, edited by David Wood and Robert Bernasconi. Evanston: Northwestern University Press, 1988.

Descartes, René. *Discourse on Method*. Translated by Laurence J. Lafleur. Indianapolis: Bobbs-Merrill, 1977.

Diderot, Denis, ed. *Encyclopédie, ou dictionnaire raisonné, des sciences, des arts et des métiers*. 36 vols. Geneva: Pellet, 1777–1779.

Dimier, Louis. *Les maitres de la contre-révolution au dix-neuvième siècle*. Paris: Nouvelle librairie nationale, 1917.

Dluhosch, Eric. "The Failure of the Soviet Avant-garde." *Oppositions* 10 (Fall 1977): 31–55.

Dodds, E. R. *The Greeks and the Irrational.* Berkeley: University of California Press, 1951.

Duby, Georges. *The Chivalrous Society.* Translated by Cynthia Postan. Berkeley: University of California Press, 1977.

Dumont, François. "French Kingship and Absolute Monarchy in the Seventeenth Century." In *Louis XIV and Absolutism,* edited by Ragnhild Hatton. Columbus: Ohio State University Press, 1976.

Eco, Umberto. "Function and Sign: The Semiotics of Architecture." In *Signs, Symbols, and Architecture,* edited by Geoffrey Broadbent, Richard Bunt, and Charles Jencks. Chichester and New York: John Wiley and Sons, 1980.

Eisenstadt, S. N. *Post-Traditional Societies.* New York: Norton, 1974.

———. "Some Observations on the Dynamics of Tradition." *Comparative Studies in Society and History* 11, no. 4 (October 1969): 451–75.

Eliade, Mircea. *Myth and Reality.* Translated by Willard R. Trask, New York: Harper and Row, 1963.

Emerson, Ralph Waldo. *Nature.* Boston and New York: Houghton, Mifflin, and Co., 1883.

Erman, Adolf. *Die Literatur der Aegypter.* Leipzig: J. C. Hinrichs, 1923.

Ewen, Elizabeth. *Immigrant Women in the Land of Dollars.* New York: Monthly Review Press, 1985.

Featherstone, Mike. "In Pursuit of the Postmodern." *Theory, Culture and Society* 5, nos. 2–3 (June 1988): 195–216.

Feher, Ferenc. "Redemptive and Democratic Paradigms in Radical Politics." *Telos* 63 (Spring 1985): 147–56.

Foster, Hal, ed. *The Anti-Aesthetic.* Port Townsend, Wash.: Bay Press, 1983.

Foucault, Michel. *Discipline and Punish.* Translated by Alan Sheridan. New York: Vintage, 1979.

———. "Nietzsche, Genealogy, History." *Language, Counter-Memory, Practice.* Edited by Donald F. Bouchard. Ithaca: Cornell University Press, 1977.

Freud, Sigmund. *Group Psychology and the Analysis of the Ego.* Translated by James Strachey. New York: Bantam, 1965.

Freyer, Hans. *Theorie des gegenwärtigen Zeitalters.* Stuttgart: Deutsche Verlags-Anstalt, 1956.

Frisby, David. "Georg Simmel: First Sociologist of Modernity." *Theory, Culture and Society* 2, no. 3 (1985): 49–67.

Gadamer, Hans-Georg. "On the Scope and Function of Hermeneutical Reflection." *Continuum* 8, nos. 1–2 (Spring-Summer 1970): 77–95.

———. "The Problem of Historical Consciousness." In *Interpretative Social Science,* edited by Paul Rabinow and William W. Sullivan. Berkeley: University of California Press, 1979.

———. *Truth and Method.* Translated by Garrett Barden and John Cumming. New York: Crossroad, 1965.

Gans, Herbert. "Symbolic Ethnicity: The Future of Ethnic Groups and Cultures in America." *Ethnic and Racial Studies* 2, no. 1 (January 1979): 1–20.

Geertz, Clifford. "The Uses of Diversity." *Michigan Quarterly Review* 25, no. 1 (Winter 1986): 105–23.

Gehlen, Arnold. *Man: His Nature and Place in the World.* Translated by Clare McMillan and Karl Pillemer. New York: Columbia University Press, 1988.

———. *Moral und Hypermoral: Eine pluralische Ethik.* Frankfurt: Athenäum Verlag, 1969.

George, Charles, and Katherine George. "Protestantism and Capitalism in Pre-Revolutionary England." In *The Protestant Ethic and Modernization,* edited by S. N. Eisenstadt. New York: Basic Books, 1968.

Giddens, Anthony. *The Consequences of Modernity.* Stanford: Stanford University Press, 1990.

Gierke, Otto von. *Natural Law and the Theory of Society, 1500–1800.* Translated by Ernest Barker. Cambridge: Cambridge University Press, 1934.

Goldmann, Lucien. *Immanuel Kant.* London: New Left Books, 1971.

Gonzales, Moishe. "Theoretical Amnesia." *Telos* 65 (Fall 1985): 163–70.

Goody, Jack. *Domestication of the Savage Mind.* Cambridge: Cambridge University Press, 1977.

———. *The Logic of Writing and the Organization of Society.* Cambridge: Cambridge University Press, 1986.

Gossman, Lionel. "History as Decipherment: Romantic Historiography and the Discourse of the Other." *New Literary History* 18, no. 1 (Autumn 1986): 23–57.

Groningen, Bernhard. *In the Grip of the Past: An Essay on Greek Thought.* Leiden: E. J. Brill, 1953.

Gross, David. "Bergson, Proust, and the Revaluation of Memory." *International Philosophical Quarterly* 25 (December 1985): 369–80.

———. "Critical Synthesis on Urban Knowledge: Remembering and Forgetting in the Modern City." *Social Epistemology* 4, no. 1 (1990): 3–22.

———. "Max Weber in Context: The Dilemmas of Modernity." *Telos* 78 (Winter 1988–89): 109–17.

———. "Rescuing the Past." *Telos* 86 (Winter 1990–91): 23–32.

———. "Space, Time and Modern Culture." *Telos* 50 (Winter 1981–82): 59–78.

———. "Temporality and the Modern State." *Theory and Society* 14, (1985): 53–82.

Gusfield, Joseph R. "Tradition and Modernity: Polarities in the Study of Social Change." *American Journal of Sociology* 72, no. 4 (January 1967): 351–62.

Habermas, Jürgen. "The Dialectics of Rationalization: An Interview with Jürgen Habermas." Interview with Alex Honneth, Eberhard Knödler-Bunte, and Arno Widmann. *Telos* 49 (Fall 1981): 5–31.

———. *Legitimation Crisis.* Translated by Thomas McCarthy. Boston: Beacon Press, 1975.

———. "Modernity and Postmodernity." *New German Critique* 22 (Winter 1981): 3–14.

———. "The New Obscurity." *Philosophy and Social Criticism* 11, no. 2 (Winter 1986): 1–18.

———. *The Philosophical Discourse of Modernity.* Translated by Frederick Lawrence. Cambridge: MIT Press, 1987.

———. "A Review of Gadamer's *Truth and Method.*" In *Understanding and Social*

Inquiry, edited by Fred R. Dallmayr and Thomas A. McCarthy. Notre Dame: Notre Dame University Press, 1977.

———. *The Theory of Communicative Action*. 2 vols. Translated by Thomas McCarthy. Boston: Beacon Press, 1984–87.

Hajda, Lubomyr, and Mark Beissinger, eds. *The Nationalities Factor in Soviet Politics and Society*. Boulder: Westview Press, 1990.

Halbwachs, Maurice. *Les cadres sociaux de la mémoire*. Paris: Presses universitaires de France, 1952.

Hallie, Philip P. *Lest Innocent Blood Be Shed*. New York: Harper and Row, 1975.

Hamann, Richard, and Jost Hermand. *Stilkunst um 1900*. Vol. 4, *Epochen deutscher Kultur von 1870 bis zur Gegenwart*. Frankfurt: Fischer Verlag, 1977.

Hart, James. "Toward a Phenomenology of Nostalgia." *Man and World* 6 (1973): 397–420.

Heller, Erich. *In the Age of Prose*. Cambridge: Cambridge University Press, 1984.

Hennis, Wilhelm. *Max Weber: Essays in Reconstruction*. Translated by Keith Tribe. London and Boston: Allen and Unwin, 1988.

Hirschman, Albert O. *The Passions and the Interests: Political Arguments for Capitalism Before Its Triumph*. Princeton: Princeton University Press, 1977.

Hobbes, Thomas. *Leviathan*. New York: E. P. Dutton, 1950.

Hobsbawm, Eric. "Introduction: Inventing Traditions." In *The Invention of Tradition*, edited by Eric Hobsbawm and Terence Ranger. Cambridge: Cambridge University Press, 1988.

———. *Labouring Men: Studies in the History of Labour*. London: Weidenfeld and Nicolson, 1964.

———. "Peasants and Politics." *Journal of Peasant Studies* 1, no. 1 (1973): 3–22.

Hoesterey, Ingeborg, ed. *Zeitgeist in Babel: The Postmodernist Controversy*. Bloomington: University of Indiana Press, 1991.

Hofer, Johannes. "Medical Dissertation on Nostalgia." Translated by Carolyn K. Anspach. *Bulletin of the History of Medicine* 2 (1934): 374–91.

Hölderlin, Friedrich. *Briefe*. Edited by Adolf Beck. Vol. 6 in *Friedrich Hölderlin: Samtliche Werke*. Edited by Friedrich Beissner. Stuttgart: Kohlhammer Verlag, 1954.

Hönig, Alois. "Zur geschichtsphilosophischen Kategorie Tradition." *Deutsche Zeitschrift für Philosophie* 12, no. 1 (1964): 1055–72.

Huyssen, Andreas. *After the Great Divide: Modernism, Mass Culture, and Postmodernism*. Bloomington: University of Indiana Press, 1986.

Jameson, Fredric. "Marxism and Historicism." *New Literary History* 11, no. 1 (Autumn 1979): 41–73.

———. *The Political Unconscious*. Ithaca: Cornell University Press, 1981.

———. "Postmodernism, or the Cultural Logic of Late Capitalism." *New Left Review* 146 (July-August 1984): 53–92.

Jennings, Bruce. "Tradition and the Politics of Remembering." *Georgia Review* 36, no. 1 (Spring 1982): 167–82.

Kamper, Dietmar, and Willem van Reijen, eds. *Der unvollendete Vernunft: Moderne versus Postmoderne*. Frankfurt: Suhrkamp, 1987.

164

Kant, Immanuel. "What Is Enlightenment?" In *The Enlightenment: A Comprehensive Anthology*, edited by Peter Gay. New York: Simon and Schuster, 1973.

Kaplan, E. Ann, ed. *Postmodernism and Its Discontents*. London: Verso, 1988.

Kautsky, John. *The Political Consequences of Modernization*. New York: Wiley, 1972.

Kellner, Douglas. "Postmodernism as Social Theory." *Theory, Culture and Society* 5, nos. 2–3 (June 1988): 239–69.

Kiesewetter, Hubert. *Industrielle Revolution in Deutschland, 1815–1914*. Frankfurt: Suhrkamp, 1980.

Kisiel, Theodore. "The Happening of Tradition: The Hermeneutics of Gadamer and Heidegger." *Man and World* 2 (August 1969): 358–85.

Klages, Ludwig. *Der Geist als Widersacher der Seele*. Leipzig: J. A. Barth, 1929.

Koselleck, Reinhart. *Futures Past: On the Semantics of Historical Time*. Translated by Keith Tribe. Cambridge: MIT Press, 1985.

Krieger, Leonard. *The Meaning of History*. Chicago: University of Chicago Press, 1977.

Kubler, George. *The Shape of Time*. New Haven: Yale University Press, 1979.

Kundera, Milan. "The Tragedy of Central Europe." *New York Review of Books*, April 26, 1984, pp. 33–39.

LaPlanche, J., and J.-B. Pontalis. *The Language of Psycho-Analysis*. Translated by Donald Nicholson-Smith. London: Hogarth Press, 1973.

Lears, T. J. Jackson. *No Place of Grace: Antimodernism and the Transformation of American Culture, 1880–1920*. New York: Pantheon, 1981.

Lefebvre, Henri. *Everyday Life in the Modern World*. Translated by Sacha Rabinovitch. New York: Harper and Row, 1971.

Leiss, William, Stephen Kline, and Sut Jhally. *Social Communication in Advertising*. Toronto and New York: Methuen, 1986.

Lewis, R.W.B. *The American Adam*. Chicago: University of Chicago Press, 1955.

Leymore, Varda Langholz. *Hidden Myth: Structure and Symbolism in Advertising*. New York: Basic Books, 1975.

Leyser, K. "The German Aristocracy from the Ninth to the Early Twelfth Century." *Past and Present* 41 (December 1968): 25–53.

Liebersohn, Harry. *Fate and Utopia in German Sociology, 1870–1923*. Cambridge: MIT Press, 1988.

Locke, John. "Second Treatise on Government." In *Treatise of Civil Government*, edited by Charles L. Sherman. New York: Appleton-Century-Crofts, 1965.

Lowe, Donald M. *History of Bourgeois Perception*. Chicago: University of Chicago Press, 1982.

Lowenthal, David. *The Past Is a Foreign Country*. New York: Cambridge University Press, 1965.

Lyotard, Jean-François. *Économie libidinale*. Paris: Éditions de minuit, 1974.

McClelland, David. *The Achieving Society*. New York: Irvington, 1976.

McIntyre, Alisdair. *Whose Justice? Whose Rationality?* Notre Dame: University of Notre Dame, 1988.

MacMullen, Ramsay. *Christianity and the Roman Empire (A.D. 100–400)*. New Haven: Yale University Press, 1984.

Machiavelli, Niccolo. *The Discourses of Niccolo Machiavelli*. Translated and annotated by Leslie J. Walker. London: Routledge and Kegan Paul, 1950.

Mannheim, Karl. "Das Problem des Generationen." *Wissenssoziologie*. Edited by Kurt H. Wolff. Berlin and Neuwied: Luchterhand, 1964.

Marchand, Roland. *Advertising and the American Dream: Making Way for Modernity, 1920–1940*. Berkeley: University of California Press, 1985.

Mauzi, Robert. *L'idée du bonheur dans la littérature et la pensée françaises au XVIIIᵉ siècle*. Paris: Librairie Armand Colin, 1960.

Meinecke, Friedrich. *Cosmopolitanism and the National State*. Translated by Robert B. Kimber. Princeton: Princeton University Press, 1970.

———. *Historicism: The Rise of a New Historical Outlook*. Translated by J. E. Anderson. London: Routledge and Kegan Paul, 1972.

Meyrowitz, Joshua. *No Sense of Place: The Impact of the Electronic Media on Social Behavior*. New York: Oxford University Press, 1985.

Michels, Robert. *Political Parties: A Sociological Study of the Oligarchical Tendencies of Modern Democracies*. Translated by Eden Paul and Cedar Paul. New York: Collier, 1962.

Milosz, Czeslaw. "An Interview with Czeslaw Milosz." *New York Review of Books*, February 27, 1986, pp. 34–35.

Mitzman, Arthur. *The Iron Cage: An Historical Interpretation of Max Weber*. New Brunswick: Transaction Books, 1985.

Mommsen, Wolfgang. "Personal Conduct and Societal Change." In *Max Weber: Rationality and Modernity*, edited by Scott Lash and Sam Whimster. London: Allen and Unwin, 1987.

Mosse, George L. *The Crisis of German Ideology*. New York: Grosset and Dunlap, 1964.

———. "Mass Politics and the Political Liturgy of Nationalism." In *Nationalism: The Nature and Evolution of an Ideal*, edited by Eugene Kamenka. London: St. Martin's Press, 1976

———. *The Nationalization of the Masses*. New York: Howard Fertig, 1975.

Mousnier, Roland. *Les Institutions de la France sous la monarchie absolue, 1598–1789*. 2 vols. Paris: Presses universitaires de France, 1974–1980.

Navari, Cornelia. "The Origins of the Nation-State." In *The Nation-State*, edited by Leonard Tivey. New York: St. Martin's Press, 1981.

Nietzsche, Friedrich. *The Gay Science*. Translated by Walter Kaufmann. New York: Vintage Press, 1974.

———. *The Portable Nietzsche*. Translated by Walter Kaufmann. New York: Viking Press, 1962.

———. *The Use and Abuse of History*. Translated by Adrian Collins. Indianapolis: Bobbs-Merrill, 1957.

Nordau, Max. *Die conventionellen Lügen der Kulturmenschheit*. Leipzig: B. Schlicke Verlag, 1884.

Oakes, Guy. "Farewell to the Protestant Ethic?" *Telos* 78 (Winter 1988–89): 81–94.

Oestreich, Gerhard. *Geist und Gestalt des frühmodernen Staates*. Berlin: Duncker and Humblot, 1969.

Offe, Claus. *Contradictions of the Welfare State*. Edited by John Keane. Cambridge: MIT Press, 1984.

———. "New Social Movements: Challenge to Boundaries of Institutional Politics." *Social Research* 52, no. 4 (Winter 1985): 817–68.

Ogilvy, James. *Many Dimensional Man: Decentralizing Self, Society, and the Sacred*. New York: Oxford University Press, 1977.

Panofsky, Erwin. *Renaissance and Renascences in Western Art*. Stockholm: Almquist and Wicksel, 1965.

Parker, David. *The Making of French Absolutism*. New York: St. Martin's Press, 1983.

Payne, Henry C. *The Philosophes and the People*. New Haven: Yale University Press, 1976.

Pelikan, Jaroslav. *Obedient Rebels: Catholic Substance and Protestant Principle in Luther's Reformation*. New York: Harper and Row, 1964.

Pellicani, Luciano. "Weber and the Myth of Calvinism." *Telos* 75 (Summer 1988): 57–85.

Pernoud, Régine. *Histoire de la bourgeoisie en France*, vol. 1. Paris: Éditions du Seuil, 1960.

Pieper, Josef. *Über den Begriff der Tradition*. Cologne and Opladen: Westdeutscher Verlag, 1958.

———. *Überlieferung*. Munich: Kösel Verlag, 1970.

Pinder, Wilhelm. *Das Problem der Generationen in der Kunstgeschichte Europas*. Berlin: Frankfurter Verlags-Anstalt, 1926.

Pocock, J.G.A. *The Machiavellian Moment: Florentine Political Thought and the Atlantic Republican Tradition*. Princeton: Princeton University Press, 1975.

———. *Politics, Language, and Time: Essays on Political Thought and History*. New York: Atheneum, 1971.

Poggi, Gianfranco. *The Development of the Modern State*. Stanford: Stanford University Press, 1978.

Popper, Karl. "Toward a Rational Theory of Tradition." *Conjectures and Refutations*. New York: Harper and Row, 1968.

Pufendorf, Samuel. *Of the Law of Nature and Nations*. 2d ed. Translated by Basil Kennett. Oxford: A. and J. Churchil, 1710.

Rabinbach, Anson. "Benjamin, Bloch and Modern German Jewish Messianism." *New German Critique* 34 (Winter 1985): 78–124.

Radin, Max. "Tradition." *Encyclopaedia of the Social Sciences*, vol. 15. Edited by Edwin Seligman. New York: Macmillan, 1937.

Raeff, Marc. *The Well-Ordered Police State*. New Haven: Yale University Press, 1983.

———. "The Well-Ordered Police State and the Development of Modernity in Seventeenth- and Eighteenth-Century Europe." *American Historical Review* 80, no. 5 (December 1975): 1221–43.

Ro'i, Yaacov, and Avi Beker, eds. *Jewish Culture and Identity in the Soviet Union.* New York: New York University Press, 1991.

Rosenberg, Hans. *Bureaucracy, Aristocracy, and Autocracy: The Prussian Experience, 1660–1815.* Boston: Beacon Press, 1966.

Runciman, Steven. *The Medieval Manichee: A Study of the Christian Dualist Heresy.* New York: Viking Press, 1961.

Rüstow, Alexander. "Kulturtradition und Kulturkritik." *Studium Generale* 9, no. 6 (June 1951): 307–11.

Said, Edward. *Beginnings: Intention and Method.* New York: Basic Books, 1975.

Schluchter, Wolfgang. *The Rise of Western Rationalism: Max Weber's Developmental Theory.* Translated by Guenter Roth. Berkeley: University of California Press, 1981.

Scholem, Gershom. *The Messianic Idea in Judaism.* New York: Schocken, 1971.

———. *Sabbatai Sevi: The Mystical Messiah, 1626–1676.* Translated by R.J.Z. Werblowsky. Princeton: Princeton University Press, 1973.

Schöpflin, George. "Nationality in Yugoslav Politics." *Survey* 25, no. 3 (Summer 1980): 1–19.

Schutz, Alfred. *The Phenomenology of the Social World.* Translated by George Walsh and Frederick Lehnert. Evanston: Northwestern University Press, 1967.

Schutz, Alfred, and Thomas Luckmann. *The Structure of the Life-World.* Translated by Richard Zaner and H. Tristram Engelhardt, Jr. Evanston: Northwestern University Press, 1973.

Shattuck, Roger. *The Innocent Eye: On Modern Literature and the Arts.* New York: Farrar, Straus, and Giroux, 1984.

Sheehan, James, ed. *Heidegger: The Man and the Thinker.* Chicago: Precedent Press, 1981.

Shils, Edward. *Tradition.* London: Faber and Faber, 1981.

Shklar, Judith. "Subversive Genealogies." *Daedalus* 101 (Winter 1972): 129–54.

Sieburth, Richard. "Introduction." *Friedrich Hölderlin: Hymns and Fragments.* Princeton: Princeton University Press, 1984.

Simmel, Georg. *The Philosophy of Money.* Translated by Tom Bottomore and David Frisby. London: Routledge and Kegan Paul, 1978.

———. "The Metropolis and Mental Life." *The Sociology of Georg Simmel.* Translated and edited by Kurt H. Wolff. Glencoe: The Free Press, 1964.

Sironneau, Jean-Pierre. *Sécularisation et religions politique.* The Hague: Mouton, 1962.

Smelser, Niel J. "The Modernization of Social Relations." In *Modernization: The Dynamics of Growth,* edited by Myron Weiner. New York: Basic Books, 1966.

Smith, Anthony. *The Ethnic Origins of Nations.* New York: Basil Blackwell, 1986.

———. *Theories of Nationalism.* New York: Harper and Row, 1971.

Sombart, Werner. *Der Bourgeois: Zur Geistesgeschichte des modernen Wirtschaftsmenschen.* Munich: Duncker and Humblot, 1913.

Speier, Hans. "The Communication of Hidden Meaning." In *Propaganda and*

Communication in World History, edited by Harold D. Lasswell, Daniel Lerner, and Hans Speier. Honolulu: University of Hawaii Press, 1980.

Sternhell, Zeev. *La droite révolutionnaire, 1885–1914: les origines françaises du fascisme*. Paris: Éditions du Seuil, 1978.

Stock, Brian. *Implications of Literacy: Written Language and Models of Interpretation in the Eleventh and Twelfth Centuries*. Princeton: Princeton University Press, 1983.

———. *Listening for the Text: On the Uses of the Past*. Baltimore: Johns Hopkins University Press, 1990.

Strauss, Leo. *Persecution and the Art of Writing*. Glencoe: The Free Press, 1952.

Sullivan, William M. *Reconstructing Public Philosophy*. Berkeley: University of California Press, 1982.

Taylor, Mark C. *Altarity*. Chicago: University of Chicago Press, 1987.

Tellenbach, Gerd. "Vom karolingischen Reichsadel zum deutschen Reichsfürstenstand." *Herrschaft und Staat in Mittelalter*. Darmstadt: Wege der Forschung, 1956.

Théofilakis, Élie, ed. *Modernes et Après? "Les Immatériaux."* Paris: Éditions autrement, 1985.

Thistlethwaite, Frank. "Migrations from Europe Overseas in the Nineteenth and Twentieth Centuries." In *Population Movements in Modern European History*, edited by Herbert Moller. New York: Macmillan, 1964.

Tocqueville, Alexis de. *Democracy in America*, vol. 2. Henry Reeve text. Edited by Phillips Bradley. New York: Knopf, 1946.

Tranter, N. L. *Population and Society, 1750–1940*. London and New York: Longman, 1985.

Ulmer, Gregory. *Applied Grammatology*. Baltimore: Johns Hopkins University Press, 1985.

Vattimo, Gianni. *The End of Modernity: Nihilism and Hermeneutics in Postmodern Culture*. Translated by Jon R. Snyder. Baltimore: Johns Hopkins University Press, 1988.

Vernant, Jean-Pierre. *Myth and Thought among the Greeks*. London: Routledge and Kegan Paul, 1983.

Vovelle, Michel. "Popular Religion." *Ideologies and Mentalities*. Translated by Eamon O'Flaherty. Chicago: University of Chicago Press, 1990.

Warren, Mark. *Nietzsche and Political Thought*. Cambridge: MIT Press, 1988.

Weber, Eugen, ed. *Paths to the Present: Aspects of European Thought from Romanticism to Existentialism*. New York: Dodd, Mead, and Co., 1966.

———. *Peasants into Frenchmen: The Modernization of Rural France, 1870–1914*. Stanford: Stanford University Press, 1976.

Weber, Max. *Economy and Society*, vol. 1. Edited by Guenther Roth and Claus Wittich. Translated by Ephraim Fischoff. Berkeley: University of California Press, 1978.

———. *The Protestant Ethic and the Spirit of Capitalism*. Translated by Talcott Parsons. New York: Scribner's, 1958.

Weinsheimer, Joel C. *Gadamer's Hermeneutics: A Reading of 'Truth and Method.'* New Haven: Yale University Press, 1985.

Werner, Karl Ferdinand. "Untersuchungen zur Frühzeit des französischen Fürstentums (9.-10. Jahrhundert)." *Die Welt als Geschichte* 17 (1958): 256–89; 19 (1959): 146–93; 20 (1960): 87–119.

Whitebook, Joel. "The Politics of Redemption." *Telos* 63 (Spring 1985): 156–68.

Whitney, Charles. *Francis Bacon and Modernity.* New Haven: Yale University Press, 1986.

Willcox, Walter, ed. *International Migrations,* vol. 1. New York, London, and Paris: Gordon and Breach, 1969.

Wolin, Richard. "Against Adjustment." *Telos* 65 (Fall 1985): 158–63.

———. "Critical Theory and the Dialectics of Rationalism." *New German Critique* 41 (Spring-Summer 1987): 23–52.

———. "Modernism and Postmodernism." *Telos* 62 (Winter 1984–85): 9–29.

———. "Utopia, Mimesis, and Reconciliation: A Redemptive Critique of Adorno's *Aesthetic Theory*." *Representations* 32 (Fall 1990): 33–49.

Yerushalmi, Yosef Hayim. *Zakhor: Jewish History and Jewish Memory.* Seattle and London: University of Washington Press, 1982.

Zipes, Jack. *Breaking the Magic Spell: Radical Theories of Folk and Fairy Tales.* Austin: University of Texas Press, 1979.

Index

INDEX

*Revue du traditionisme français et
étranger,* 81
Riehl, Wilhelm Heinrich, 150
Rilke, Rainer Maria, 50
Roby, John, 150
Roman Law, 9
Romanticism, 50, 149
Rudorff, Ernst, 49
Russia, 32, 44, 69. *See also* U.S.S.R.
Ryan, Michael, 154

Saint Dominic, 140
Saint Francis, 140
Sébillot, Paul, 150
Seeley, John, 82
Self, notions of: in early capitalism,
    29–30; in later capitalism, 52–53;
    in modernism, 60; in modernity, 40,
    51–52; in postmodernism, 60
Simmel, Georg, 145
Social Contract, 27
Solidarity Movement (Poland), 125
Sombart, Werner, 29, 52
Spain, 32
Spanish Civil War, 125
Spivak, Gayatri Chakravorty, 154
State, 5, 30–34, 42–49, 53, 63–64, 67,
    68–72, 79, 82, 90, 91, 107–10, 111,
    112–13, 114, 116, 118, 119, 121,
    123, 124, 126, 128, 131, 144; bu-
    reaucratic tendencies in, 44–49;
    centralization of, 31–34; and crisis
    management, 68; and crisis of legit-
    imacy, 69; and images, 112–13; and
    rationalization, 33–34, 45–49, 53,
    144; relation to tradition, 44–47, 53,
    63–64, 67, 68–72, 82, 90, 91, 107–
    10, 112–13, 116, 118, 119, 121,
    123, 124, 126, 131; types of, 30–34
Surrealism, 54
Switzerland, 71
Sybel, Heinrich von, 82
Symbolism, 54

Taylor, Frederick W., 48
Television, 57–59, 73

Thiers, Adolphe, 82
Tocqueville, Alexis de, 143
Torah, 156
Totem and Taboo (Freud), 9
Tradition: and absolutist state, 30–34,
    44, 140–41; "aura" of, 96–98, 102,
    118–19; and capitalism, 5, 7, 28–30,
    37–39, 42–47, 63–64, 67–68, 72–
    76, 78, 90–91, 94, 107–8, 109–10,
    111, 112–13, 114, 118–19, 121,
    122, 123; compared to customs, 12–
    13; and concept of "beginning
    again," 26–28, 139; consequences
    of decline of, 3–4, 62–63, 131–32;
    and creativity, 4, 24, 35, 55, 56, 129;
    critical possibilities of, 5–6, 7, 16,
    18–19, 78, 83–91, 99–101, 105–6,
    113, 117–19, 128–29, 132–35, 140,
    152; and deconstruction, 113–16;
    definitions of, 8–12; dialoguing
    with, 14–15, 93, 101–6; and empiri-
    cism, 23–25; Enlightenment attack
    on, 34–37; and ethics, 63, 96, 129,
    151; function of, 3, 6, 9–10, 20–21,
    63, 81, 83; and genealogy, 116–19;
    and images, 58, 74–76, 111–13,
    120; and immanent critique, 132–
    35; and individualism, 4, 29–30; in-
    ventions of, 71–72, 75–76, 148; and
    modern state, 5, 7, 37, 42–47, 63–
    64, 67, 68–72, 76, 78, 90–91, 94,
    107–8, 109–10, 111, 112–13, 114,
    118–19, 121, 122, 123; modes of
    transmission, 10–13, 15–19, 23,
    110, 127, 156; need for, 7, 64–68,
    73, 90–91, 121; and noncontem-
    poraneity, 93–96, 98, 99, 100, 101,
    104, 105, 129; and nostalgia, 75–76,
    148–49; and otherness, 83–87, 88,
    89, 92, 98, 100, 101, 102, 103, 105,
    106; problems of transmission, 10–
    12, 13–15, 16–18, 21–23, 127, 138,
    153, 155, 156; and rationalism, 23–
    25; refunctioning of, 107–10, 111,
    113, 114, 115, 116, 117–18, 153,
    155; and relation to "origins," 21, 26,

174